NEW WILD
garden

Natural-style planting and practicalities

NEW WILD
garden

Natural-style planting and practicalities

Ian Hodgson

for Judith

Frances Lincoln Limited
74–77 White Lion Street
Islington N1 9PF

New Wild Garden
Copyright © Frances
Lincoln Limited 2016
Text copyright ©
Ian Hodgson 2016
Photographs: copyright ©
see page 176
First Frances Lincoln
edition 2016

Edited by Zia Allaway
Designed by Becky Clarke

A catalogue record for this
book is available from the
British Library

ISBN 978-0-7112-3728-5
Printed in China

9 8 7 6 5 4 3 2 1

Quarto is the authority on a wide
range of topics.

Quarto educates, entertains
and enriches the lives of our
readers – enthusiasts and lovers
of hands-on living.

www.QuartoKnows.com

PAGE 2 Early-summer-flowering alliums mingle with salvias and grassses to provide a feast for pollinating insects.

RIGHT Borders filled with a diverse mix of flowers, grasses, and shrubs make a rich habitat for wildlife.

contents

introduction

ABOVE Meadows filled with annual field poppies and dog daisies make a spectacular display at sunset. Such landscapes were once commonplace in Britain and elsewhere, but modern agricultural methods have made them a rare sight today.

IF GARDENS ARE A REFLECTION of human intent and mirror social change, then a significant revolution has taken place over the past few years. This new perspective has not been driven solely by a desire to change the appearance of gardens from a purely visual standpoint, but also from a profound longing to re-engage with nature and work with it, rather than against it. We also want to reference many of the plant communities we see in the wild and reformulate them in our gardens in new and refreshing ways. Utilising native or exotic plants, or mixtures of both, from trees through to bulbs and diminutive annuals, these naturalistic designs are now available to all, whatever the size of your plot. Other schemes look to semi-natural communities, such as grasslands, augmenting them with seasonal flowers to produce dramatic effects.

As well as using naturalistic planting, there is also a drive to create gardens that are more in tune with natural processes, and, more importantly, our local conditions. Plants most appropriate for the site's soil and microclimate, and those that make good neighbours, are chosen for these schemes, so that the communities we create are better able to sustain themselves. Ensuring that our selected plants flourish and matching them to the local conditions also helps to minimise maintenance, such as mowing and weeding, thereby reducing the need for chemicals and fuel. That said, no artificial plant community is completely maintenance-free and some schemes may require considerable investment in time and effort to establish or require new ways of working to ensure success.

Nature's way

Taking our cue from nature encourages a more considered and efficient use of natural and manufactured resources so that ultimately our gardens tread lightly on the earth. While this may not appear to generate huge savings in individual gardens, collectively it can make a significant difference.

Gardens can also be potent catalysts for change by making political and socio-economic statements and by providing a valuable habitat

for wildlife they really do make an important contribution. With habitats in the wider landscape under threat from development, agriculture and human interference, gardens offer refuges and sources of food for a wide range of birds, insects, small mammals, reptiles and amphibians, often at critical times of the year. Even the most modest investments we make can be of immense value. Whether it is simply growing plants known to provide food for pollinating insects and birds, or creating habitats, such as introducing water for amphibians, letting the grass grow longer for insects and invertebrates, or increasing the amount of shrub cover for birdlife, the collective contribution is of huge value.

This book aims to present a range of garden and landscape effects in clearly defined chapters, so that you can follow the ideas and examples to establish similar schemes in your own outdoor space.

ABOVE LEFT The pale purple cone flower *Echinacea pallida* and butterfly weed *Asclepias tuberosa* that combine harmoniously in prairie meadows in the American Midwest have inspired designers to imitate these habitats to produce sustainable planting schemes.

ABOVE RIGHT *Aster alpinus* and *Campanula scheuchzeri* luxuriate in a moist alpine meadow in Switzerland. Garden situations, from border edgings through to domestic roof gardens, can mimic this natural habitat.

ABOVE Shade cast by trees, shrubs or buildings offers planting opportunities based on wild plant communities, such as this tranquil English woodland full of bluebells (*Hyacinthoides non-scripta*).

creating naturalistic landscapes 1

Besides having a timeless beauty, grassland is also a valuable habitat for many kinds of insect and invertebrates. The distinction between short mown turf and longer grass also exerts a dynamic rhythm that can be tailored to suit any space.

inspiring natural landscapes

With the preservation of natural habitats and wildlife essential to our planet's future survival, it is now widely recognised that home gardeners can collectively play a major role in the conservation of our precious flora and fauna.

Reconnecting with nature

Recent years have seen a significant rise in the global interest in wild landscapes and there has been a major drive to preserve and maintain them. This change in attitude is largely borne out of a desire to reconnect with nature and a concern for the future existence and well-being of these wild places, as increased expansion of urban, agricultural and industrial developments demand more space, taking their toll on fragile ecosystems. Fragmentation and destruction of wildlife habitats has displaced many organisms, which now have to survive in dwindling areas of natural space, their existence often balanced on a knife-edge as the tide of destruction continues.

The plight of bees and loss of other pollinators has brought into sharp focus our dependence on the wildlife around us; without pollination many crops would fail catastrophically, with serious implications for our future survival. With an estimated worth of around £690 million in the UK alone and £120 billion worldwide, over 80 per cent of crops, including fruit, vegetables and plants grown for their oils, such as sunflowers and rape, depend on insect pollinators. Meanwhile, research by the charity Butterfly Conservation indicates that six common butterflies in the UK could become extinct by 2050 due to a combination of drought caused by climate change and habitat loss.

TOP RIGHT A grassy meadow full of flowers is a captivating sight and a feature that has long inspired gardeners and designers around the world. The choice and type of wildflowers used in such plantings can be adapted to suit a wide range of garden conditions.

BOTTOM RIGHT Water is a powerful and important element in any wild garden. A magnet for wildlife, it provides a breeding ground for amphibians and a place to bathe and drink for birds, but features do not need to be large to make good habitats.

BELOW Narrow steps weave through a tumble of shrubs from Mediterranean climates in this sunny, sheltered, hillside garden. Yellow *Phlomis longifolia*, blue *Ceanothus thyrsiflorus* var *repens* and a maroon-blotched rock rose *Cistus ladanifer* thrive in the well-drained soil, providing colourful summer highlights.

Reflecting ecological principles

Nature is an important aesthetic and technical role model for those of us wishing to recreate a natural environment in our gardens. When looking to natural landscapes for inspiration, we need to take into account that some, such as pristine deciduous woodland and prairie grassland, comprise the native vegetation that has evolved in that particular climate, while others, including meadow grassland, field hedgerows and coppiced woodland, which we may think of as natural, have in fact been altered and manipulated by man over thousands of years. Historically, the agricultural techniques used to create these man-made landscapes worked in sympathy with natural processes and allowed the plant communities we now cherish to evolve and

adapt. But in recent years, the demands of intensive food production and use of modern machinery, along with the liberal spraying of pesticides and herbicides, have erased many of these special habitats.

While the agricultural industry grapples with ways of integrating nature back into farming practices, as gardeners we can harness the ecological principles and techniques that underpin both native and man-made plant communities to create beautiful spaces that are in tune with and support wildlife and the environment. By studying natural landscapes, and matching those with similar site and soil conditions to your own, you can recreate these habitats at home. You can also employ a number of planting and design techniques that take inspiration from nature, but have been adapted for garden settings.

BELOW A grassy meadow dotted with ox-eye daisies, *Leucanthemum vulgare*, creates a tranquil scene. This adaptable species is useful in meadow mixes as it is long-flowered and naturalises well. For a uniform visual statement it is unsurpassed, but you can also grow it with other species.

naturalistic planting designs

THE HIGH PROFILE WORK of influential designers in Holland, Germany, the United Kingdom and the United States has in recent years led to a meteoric rise of the planting style known as 'new naturalism'. The approach, which is both aesthetic and scientific, uses plant combinations that mimic wild landscapes, such as the American prairie and central European steppe grasslands, with herbaceous and evergreen perennials and ornamental grasses set out in bold sinuous swathes or smaller groupings.

Although a number of pioneer horticulturists and designers in Holland and Germany have developed new naturalism methods, it is the designs of Dutch nurseryman Piet Oudolf that have come to epitomise this style. Leading practitioners in the UK have also been influential, and include garden designers Tom Stuart-Smith and Dan Pearson, together with the landscape architect, Dr Nigel Dunnett of Sheffield University, who designed the planting for London's 2012 Olympic Park with his colleagues Professor James Hitchmough and garden designer Sarah Price. New methods devised by Dr Dunnett and his team, together with those by Professor Wolfram Kirchner at Anhalt University of Applied Sciences in Germany, also include wildlife conservation and water management, and these innovations are now filtering down into techniques for home gardeners.

Long-lasting effects

The proportion of ornamental grasses to perennials determines the character and performance of new naturalism style, conveying either a sweep of grassland or more colourful perennial meadow. The planting mix also affects the length of the flowering period, with late-flowering grasses and their subsequent dried stems and seed heads helping to prolong interest into winter, after the perennials are over.

Perennials are chosen for their robustness, impact, weather resistance and long performance; they also do not require staking or fertilising. As a result, once established, they need little management, save for cutting down and removing old foliage in late winter. The plants form tight clumps or creep very slowly, and are designed to gently mingle, without one more rampageous partner swamping another. Designers often inject excitement by creating different levels within the planting, with ground cover and compact forms rubbing shoulders with taller

LEFT A sumptuous border in late summer planted in prairie style, with dramatic clumps of *Miscanthus* grasses, colour provided by pink *Echinacea*, magenta *Monarda*, red *Helenium* and spiny, blue *Eryngium*, and spires of annual *Atriplex hortensis* var *rubra* providing accents at the back.

> 6 Naturalistic plantings can be freeform, like a grassland, or fitted into more formal geometric borders, and contrasted with tightly clipped hedges or topiary. 9

species and upright airy perennials and grasses. Early summer bulbs, such as alliums, are also included to elevate the drama at that time of year. Alternatively, you can create startling effects by omitting mid-height plants, leaving just ground cover, spring and summer bulbs and tall 'emergents'. And in smaller gardens, use compact or upright varieties to provide a sketch of the visual effects of larger schemes.

Naturalistic plantings can be freeform, like a grassland, or fitted into more formal geometric borders and contrasted with clipped hedges or topiary. Shrubs and trees, such as *Viburnum*, *Cotoneaster* or *Amelanchier,* can also be introduced, reflecting the way these plants grow in the natural landscape.

ABOVE *Rudbeckia* is an important long-flowering staple of prairie-style plantings, providing vibrant colours in shades of yellow and orange from summer into autumn.

OPPOSITE ABOVE Ebullient drifts of summer perennials, such as *Eupatorium* (back), pink phlox and red *Persicaria* (front) wrap around a pathway, with the ornamental grasses, *Stipa gigantea* and *Calamagrostis* providing structure and long-lasting seed heads in autumn and winter.

OPPOSITE BELOW LEFT A measured planting of herbaceous and evergreen perennials provides a controlled yet informal arrangement of texture and colour. While the distinctive flower heads of *Phlomis russeliana* make a dramatic accent, other perennials add to the colourful tapestry.

OPPOSITE BELOW RIGHT The pink species of *Echinacea purpurea* is more robust and persistent than many of the modern hybrids.

PLANTS USED IN NEW NATURALISM SCHEMES

These species and their cultivars are chosen for their long-lasting flowers and durability.

Perennials
- *Achillea filipendulina* (top left)
- *Echinacea purpurea*
- *Eupatorium maculatum*
- *Geranium* species
- *Helenium* species
- *Persicaria* species
- *Phlomis russeliana*
- *Rudbeckia* species
- *Salvia nemorosa*
- *Sanguisorba* species
- *Scabiosa* species
- *Sedum spectabile*
- *Verbascum* species

Grasses and sedges
- *Deschampsia cespitosa*
- *Festuca* species
- *Miscanthus sinensis* (middle left)
- *Molinia caerulea*
- *Panicum virgatum*
- *Stipa* species

Bulbs
- *Allium* species
- *Nectaroscordum* (bottom left)

PRECIOUS POOLS

Water is a magnet for wildlife. Just a little pool will pay huge dividends, attracting all manner of birds, small mammals, amphibians and insects in numbers far greater than you would imagine for the size of the water feature. Even a small depression that regularly fills with water will lure in these creatures, and by surrounding your pond with vegetation to provide protection and cover, numbers will increase even further. (See pp.117–119 on how to create and plant up a wildlife pond.)

making habitats for wildlife

CREATING HABITATS FOR WILDLIFE in your garden it is not as complicated as it may at first appear, and even tiny spaces can be adapted. Simply introducing plants of known interest to insects, birds and animals, and including a few key features, will attract all manner of wildlife within a surprisingly short period of time. The key to success is to integrate wildlife areas throughout the garden, taking a holistic approach, rather than setting aside a separate area, as wildlife does not acknowledge borders, barriers or zones!

Providing cover and shelter is particularly important for wildlife. Include shrubs, especially evergreens, for birds to roost and nest in, and plants that offer autumn berries, which will help to sustain wildlife through the colder months. It also pays to be slightly untidy

ABOVE Water, even if temporary, provides an important habitat for many kinds of wildlife, particularly insects. Even if they don't breed in your pond, dragonflies and mayflies are likely to be visitors, particularly if it is edged with flowering plants that offer them food and a resting place.

and less horticulturally house-proud. For example, try leaving spent flower stems on herbaceous plants over winter. These will provide hiding places for ladybirds and lacewings, whose offspring will collectively munch through next year's plague of aphids. And instead of disposing of surplus prunings or logs from lopped trees and hedges, pile them up in a secluded area to create homes for ground-dwelling beetles and other invertebrates.

Break down barriers

Fences of all kinds form a barrier for larger mammals, such as hedgehogs, but you can allow them easier access to your garden by creating a 30cm (1ft) square opening at the bottom of a panel. Or

OPPOSITE A frill of flowering plants beside a water feature will attract a whole host of pollinating insects, as well as amphibians and small mammals who will use their leafy stems as cover and shelter.

BELOW Trees and shrubs, plants that attract pollinators, and water combine to provide the full spectrum of habitats for all kinds of wildlife. Water can form the focus of a garden and if artfully designed with irregular margins it can look larger than it actually is.

create a fedge, a barrier of dead twigs and leaves formed from lengths of prunings woven together around a series of stakes. This will provide a habitat for beetles and invertebrates and can be installed as part of a hedgerow, or as a garden boundary.

Grassy homes

Allowing the grass to grow longer and native wildflowers to thrive also benefits wildlife, as many insects use this kind of habitat to lay eggs, where the flowers, seed heads, stems and leaves provide food and shelter for their larvae. Butterflies, such as ringlets, marbled whites and skippers, feed on grasses, while red admirals, peacocks and small tortoiseshells reside on nettles. Moth caterpillars also prefer grasses, as well as hedgerow plants, such as hawthorn, blackthorn and hazel, and woodland plants, including foxgloves and primulas.

DIY insect hotels

Although you can buy prefabricated 'insect hotels', there really is no need, and most will be happy in nooks and crannies that already exist in the garden. Undisturbed patches of bare earth at the base of a wall will offer a home to many types of solitary bee. These bees also like the crevices in old bricks and timberwork, and will use them to nest and rear their young. You can create more habitats for bees and other pollinating insects by binding together clusters of hollow canes or dried plant stems and inserting them into sheltered nooks.

To create more sophisticated insect hotels, buy a few galvanised metal gabions. Fill these mesh cages, which are widely available through garden centres and on the internet, with old bricks, terracotta roof tiles, plant stems, straw, old tree roots and prunings. Locate them around the garden and you will vastly extend the range of potential insect habitats. Another option is to make a low wall from logs piled on top of one another. As well as providing lots of habitat spaces, it can also be used as a retaining wall in a sloping garden if the logs are large enough. And by squeezing small alpines and hardy succulents in some of the holes between the logs, the wall will also provide pollen and nectar for bees and other insects when the plants are in bloom.

> ❝ You can create more habitats for bees and other overwintering insects by binding together clusters of hollow canes and dried plant stems and inserting them into sheltered nooks. ❞

OPPOSITE TOP LEFT Rainwater is directed beneath a deck from the downpipe of a shed to form this pool – any excess water runs into a soakaway.

OPPOSITE TOP RIGHT Even a small rain-fed pond creates a valuable habitat for frogs and other amphibians.

OPPOSITE LEFT A log pile provides a stabilising wall in this sloping garden, as well as a refuge for insects, including beetles and spiders.

TOP RIGHT A horizontal cluster of hollow dry plant stems from angelica, teasel or globe artichoke make an ideal refuge for many types of solitary bee, which use them to hibernate in during the winter and to breed.

BOTTOM RIGHT Known as a fedge, this structure of unwanted logs and pruned shrub stems creates a sturdy barrier or garden screen, and provides an array of habitats for many kinds of woodland wildlife.

❝ Research suggests that insects, such as bees, butterflies and hoverflies, are fairly indiscriminate about where their sources of pollen and nectar come from, and are just as likely to take them from exotic plants as natives. ❞

BELOW Pollinators, such as hoverflies and bees, will flock to single flowers like daisies and geraniums because the nectar and pollen is easy for them to access.

providing food for pollinators

WITH THE LOSS OF NATURAL and wildflower habitats, garden flowers are now acknowledged to be the most important sources of food for many bees and other insect pollinators. Populations of many types of bee, particularly the honey bee, have been badly hit worldwide, their decline attributed to the effects of parasites, disease and the use of pesticides, but research shows that home gardeners can help to reverse this trend by including a selection of pollen- and nectar-rich blooms.

Endless variety

Studies by the Royal Horticultural Society indicate that growing a wide diversity of flowering plants directly increases the range of pollinating insects drawn to a planted area. Their research also suggests that insects, such as bees, butterflies and hoverflies, are fairly indiscriminate about where sources of pollen and nectar come from and are just as likely to take them from exotic plants as from natives. But while growing a broad range is ideal, the main point to remember is that insects can only feed

from flowers that produce pollen and sugary nectar. Double flowers and some sterile plants have had these elements bred out, which only makes them of interest to the gardener.

Exotic plants can extend and augment the role of native species that flower in the first half of the year and are in seed by late summer. Including later-flowering exotics, such as salvias, asters and other autumnal daisies, single-flowered dahlias and late annuals, such as zinnias and cosmos, will significantly extend seasonal food supplies. At the beginning of the year, early-flowering perennials, such as wallflowers and *Pulmonaria*, and bulbs, including snowdrops and scillas, help to feed insects that come out of hibernation early. Solitary and mason bees, both important pollinators of fruit trees, are examples of these early risers.

Easy pickings

Bees and hoverflies are by far the most frequent visitors to gardens, with butterflies and other pollinating insects making up just two per cent each, according to recent studies by the University of Sussex. To redress the balance and increase the diversity of insect life in your garden, choose a range of plants that produce flowers of different shapes and sizes.

A flower's shape and structure influences the type of insect pollinator it will attract. Bees in particular like open, cup-shaped blooms, such as poppies, buttercups, single roses and *Potentilla*, which are easy to access and produce copious amounts of pollen. Many insects, including bees, also favour cranesbills (*Geranium* species), which secrete nectar from the base of the petals at the centre of the bloom, while the flower structure of members of the daisy family, such as *Anthemis, Inula, Helianthus, Centaurea* and *Eupatorium,* is made up of clusters of tiny individual blooms called disc florets which attract a whole range of insects.

The hooded or lipped flowers of the pea and sage family, such as salvia, lavender, origanum and *Phlomis*, are also highly attractive to bees, with clover (*Trifolium rubrum*) and bird's-foot-trefoil (*Lotus corniculatus*) especially valuable. In the buttercup family, *Aquilegia* and *Aconitum* are sought out by long-tongued bumblebees.

With their long proboscis or 'tongue', butterflies and moths can access narrow tubular flowers, such as *Buddleja* and members of the cabbage and pink family. Members of the carrot family, such as *Anthriscus, Daucus* and *Angelica,* feature flat-topped heads comprising masses of tiny flowers, which attract hoverflies, small beetles and small solitary bees, while gooseberry and ivy blooms are sought out by social wasps.

ABOVE The easy-to-access nectar of the purple cone flower (*Echinacea purpurea*) attracts bees and butterflies, and makes a beautiful garden plant for sites in full sun with free-draining soil.

BECOME A HOME SCIENTIST

We know surprisingly little about the value of insect pollinators and how they adapt to changes in climate and land use, but research shows that garden owners can make a vital contribution. There is a host of science projects that need volunteers to make observations about how wildlife interacts with their garden habitats, work that would be too expensive to conduct or sustain for long periods without their help. To take part in a scheme, contact your local Wildlife Trust.

LEFT Many pollinating insects, including different types of bee, have preferences for particular plant species and flower forms, so grow as wide a range as possible for the maximum benefit.

creating an eco-friendly garden

AS WELL AS CHOOSING appropriate plants, you can also make your garden more environmentally friendly by thinking carefully about how you manage, construct and develop your outdoor space.

If you want to attract and care for wildlife, it is important to restrict or stop the use of pesticides. There are many other ways of controlling pests and diseases and by including plants known to be resistant to particular diseases, such as mildews, and those that won't attract hordes of debilitating pests, you can minimise attacks.

Maintaining plant health by selecting the right plant for the right place is key, and getting to know your site conditions before making your selections (see pp.45–48) will pay dividends. If you are new to your garden, take a year or so to see how the microclimate works and, if it is a mature plot, try to identify the plants as they appear and the types of wildlife they attract, so you can assess their suitability and integrate the best into your 'wild' designs.

BELOW A semi-shaded area is transformed here into a woodland setting with primroses, bluebells and creeping plants forming an extensive ground cover, while a juneberry (*Amelanchier*) and a clematis on the fence provide flowers and foliage above. Because the plants suit the site and are healthy, they have a greater resistance to attacks by pests and diseases and therefore reduce the need for chemical pesticides.

Alternative pest controls

In recent years the range of pesticides available to home gardeners has been drastically reduced due to a range of environmental and health concerns. Organic controls, or those made from natural compounds, such as pyrethrum or pyrethroids, plant oils, fatty acids, and soaps, help to keep some pests at bay. You can also try biological controls, such as microscopic nematodes or eelworms that prey upon a range of pests, including vine weevils, cutworms, caterpillars, and slugs. If you do elect to use other chemical pesticides, always target their use to the affected plants or plant parts and only apply them when all other methods have failed.

Controlling slugs and snails to prevent them decimating emerging shoots and seedlings is a constant challenge. Again, try to use plants that they tend to avoid. Although these molluscs love the fleshy stems of lupins and delphiniums, neither of which you are likely to use in a wild garden, they also like species of *Achillea* and some campanulas, which you may wish to include. In a small plot, armed with a torch, you can pick them off by hand at night, or use a biological control or products based on ferric (iron) phosphate, which is less harmful to wildlife and the environment than metaldehyde, the component used in most slug pellets.

Recycled free resources

Compost as much green waste from your garden as possible and use when it has rotted down to improve the soil quality on vegetable and perennial beds, or as a mulch around trees and shrubs.

Harvesting rainwater is the best use of a free resource that is so often wasted. Whether you use the harvested water on your plants or for creating a wildlife pond or bog garden, or all of these, the universal benefit is that you will be preventing water from pouring down the drain as waste. A number of other ideas and opportunities for rainwater are discussed through the book (see pp.114–117).

Salvaged goods

Always try to reuse materials, such as excavated topsoil or subsoil, where possible, or find new uses for materials found on your site, such as old paving, bricks or concrete, rather than consigning it to landfill. Recycled materials and objects from salvage yards or skips offer untold opportunities for fashioning exciting features that have a timeless, weathered look. Where the appearance of timber is unimportant or you need a rustic finish, use recycled or secondhand wood, rather than buying new. Secondhand bricks and paving slabs from salvage merchants will also be ready-aged, imparting an instant sense of place and often costing much less than new materials.

CHEMICAL-FREE WEED SUPPRESSION

Laying mulches and covering the soil with leafy and ground-cover plants, such as the bark chips and sedum above, will help to reduce the need for herbicides, as they leave little space for weed seeds to fall on bare soil and germinate. Most annual weeds can be removed easily by hand or careful hoeing; try to remove them before they flower and set seed. If it proves difficult to eliminate perennial weeds, such as field thistle or bindweed, by hand, spot treat them with systemic herbicides, unless you are clearing badly infested ground which may require wider use. When using any herbicides always follow the manufacturer's instructions carefully.

selecting a natural style

THE INSPIRATIONS UNDERPINNING the creation of any natural garden are the wild places and landscapes that surround us. The basic habitat types of woodland, grassland and water comprise enormous variety in terms of the plants they support and the scale of the landscape, and while it is possible to recreate any of these habitats, your approach will depend on the space you have available.

It is also important to match your location and climate with wild landscapes that have similar conditions to ensure the plant communities you choose to develop will thrive. For instance, it's no good using forest trees in a small, urban space, but you could instead plant slender, open-canopied birch and rowan species to achieve a similar effect. Any water will attract wildlife, but it would be self-defeating to install a pool beneath a dense tree canopy where few aquatics will grow well and the water will fill with leaves every year. And if you are time poor, do not choose a meadow that requires high annual maintenance.

To succeed, use your site and situation to best effect and be realistic about what can be achieved. By following these principles you can create a beautiful wild garden that dovetails with and enhances your lifestyle and makes a positive contribution to the wider environment.

BELOW Bold clumps of *Miscanthus* grasses are enveloped by rich pink rivulets of *Echinacea* punctuated by the yellow flowers of *Rudbeckia maxima* which float above the mix in high summer. You can achieve these dramatic effects even in small spaces.

URBAN WOODLAND

This calm, contemporary oasis behind a terraced house in London is a symphony of green, created from creeper-clad fences, ferns and ornamental grasses shrouded in gentle shade from white-stemmed birches. Bulbs, such as alliums, and foxgloves, provide seasonal highlights. The trees hide the scale of the dwelling and the patio is screened from the windows of adjoining houses. Wildlife, particularly birds, will welcome the tree, climber and shrub cover, while bees will visit and feed from the selection of summer perennials.

CONTEMPORARY COTTAGE STYLE

This small cottage-style garden is specially valuable to emerging pollinators. From the appearance of bulbs in late winter and early perennials, such as *Pulmonaria*, to the informal groupings of autumn-flowering plants and shrubs, the needs of wildlife are sustained for most of the year. While some perennials and dwarf shrubs are grown for structure, annuals and short-lived perennials colonise the gaps to give a sense of riotous abandon. Seedlings of such plants can be thinned out according to need, and spares transplanted into other areas as required.

WILD WATER GARDEN

Water is the most valuable habitat you can create in your garden, supporting a wide variety of wildlife. Wild water gardening is as much about the position and design of the feature as it is about planting. Always set your pool or pond in a depression, with the outline reflecting the contours of the surrounding ground. You can then overlay a more geometric design, as shown here with a rectangular deck and bridge. Planting in the water should blend seamlessly with that in the borders edging it, while a shallow beach area will allow wildlife easy access.

❝ Increase wildlife by allowing some turf to grow longer, and perhaps naturalise bulbs, shrubs and perennials into it. You may also wish to introduce a wildflower, prairie or perennial meadow. ❞

ABOVE The agricultural landscapes surrounding this garden have inspired the use of grasses and meadows, which create a potent drama, with model sheep and golden cornfields adding to the effect.

OPPOSITE TOP LEFT A pair of staddle stones mark the transition from more formal planting into a relaxed grassy meadow with simple mown pathway.

FAR RIGHT The loose groups of grasses, sedges, and perennials that edge this stream allow annuals, such as wild carrot, to naturalise freely.

BOTTOM Perennials, such as *Rudbeckia fulgida* var *sullivantii* 'Goldsturm', *Echinacea*, *Eryngium agavifolium*, tall yellow *Helianthus maximiliani* and teasel seed heads mingle to create a colourful late summer spectacle.

transforming a large garden into a wild one

HAVING A LARGE GARDEN to transform into a wild one may seem to offer the best of all worlds, but it will still need careful thought and planning before you start. Firstly, look at the various habitats you have on site (see also pp.18–21) and whether they can be enhanced or fused with the wilder landscape beyond.

Planting trees and shrubs to create a woodland edge will pay dividends and provide valuable habitat for all kinds of wildlife, particularly birds. You could also introduce a hedgerow of native species, or perhaps include a few exotic species for their flowers. Think too about using species that provide fruit, such as thornless blackberries, edible hawthorns or juneberries, gooseberries, apples or crab apples to add extra value.

Make a meadow

Your garden probably includes some grassland that requires regular mowing. If this is the case, one of the best ways to reduce this maintenance and increase wildlife is to allow some turf to grow longer, and perhaps naturalise a few bulbs, perennials or shrubs into it (see pp.84–97). This may mean you have to cut it back with a strimmer periodically but it will dramatically reduce the mowing required. You may also wish to introduce a wildflower, prairie or perennial meadow. Such large-scale projects need careful planning, not just regarding their composition, but also the planting methods and management that will be required. If you have never undertaken such a project before, you may want to seek professional advice from an experienced practitioner or landscape designer, who can help formulate a plan and carry out the initial groundwork and establishment.

Ways with water

In general, larger or moving bodies or water are more self-sustaining than small pools. Where the site conditions support it, you could augment an existing stream, bog or pond to create a beautiful wildlife-friendly feature. Possibilities include excavating a boggy area, enlarging a small pond, or lining a depression at the bottom of a slope that can be filled with natural run-off from surrounding land. Again, before undertaking such a project, seek advice from a civil engineer or hydrologist, particularly if you plan to divert a stream or watercourse.

While a single body of water will have presence, you could also consider a series of smaller ponds of various sizes, perhaps linked by narrow channels. A diversity of edge treatments, planting zones, beach areas and water depths will attract a wider range of wildlife than you would find in just one large feature.

let nature reign in a small space

ALTHOUGH SMALL SPACES may not seem to offer the potential of larger sites, you may be surprised by how much you can achieve. Much will depend on the size of your plot, where it is located and what is going on around it. If your garden is shaded for much of the day by buildings, structures or trees, opt for a woodland style rather than meadow plantings, which are better adapted to sunny situations, although some perennial meadow-like schemes will perform well in semi-shade.

Forward planning

Assess your site carefully and map the sunny and shady areas at different times of the day and throughout the year (see p.48). You can then use this information to locate the best areas for different types of habitat and planting. You may also want to remove unwanted trees or move shrubs, or thin out or lift their canopies to allow more light to filter through to the soil below, thereby expanding your planting options. Carry out this heavy work before introducing new plants, which may be damaged in the process.

Also look for opportunities to augment what you already have, such as adding shade-tolerant plantings beneath and around trees and shrubs, diversifying a lawn area with naturalised bulbs, or leaving an area of grass to grow a little longer.

Flowers for all seasons

Ensuring pollinating insects are catered for throughout the year has an additional benefit, creating

TOP LEFT The clean lines of the minimalist timber seating in this tiny woodland glade lend a contemporary twist to the lush woodland planting.

BOTTOM LEFT An al fresco dining area around a farmhouse table and bench is backed by a raised planter filled with the bold silver spikes of *Astelia chathamica*, white alliums and creamy *Sisyrinchium striatum*.

TOP RIGHT A buddleia hedge provides a wildlife haven behind a bed thronging with the vibrant pink and white daisies of *Echinacea*, white *Anaphalis margaritacea* var *yedoensis* and purple alliums.

BOTTOM RIGHT A home for insects, the hand-crafted stone walls in this rustic Mediterranean garden are softened with a riotous jumble of drought-tolerant bee plants, such as *Phlomis*, *Nepeta*, *Eryngium*, and *Euphorbia*, and the evergreen herbs, rosemary and thyme.

a continuous flower show for you to enjoy too. This is especially important in small gardens where the whole space can usually be seen at all times. Choose a selection of spring bulbs, trees and shrubs, wildflowers, exotics and perennials for summer colour and autumn interest, and winter flowers to brighten up those gloomy months.

Watering holes

Small ponds or pools will attract a wide range of wildlife, including frogs, toads, newts and dragon- and damselflies, and they will also provide a watering hole for birds and small mammals. Many features are easily accommodated in small spaces and, when sympathetically designed, they will be an important visual asset too.

Also consider turning an ornamental pool into a rain pond by filling it with run-off from the roofs of sheds, conservatories or greenhouses; regulate water levels with an overflow connected to a soakaway, ditch or storm-water drain. Even shallow scrapes or depressions that fill with water in winter and dry out in summer will be of value and could also form the nucleus of a small bog garden.

Neighbourhood links

If your garden is not too tiny, you could include a little bit of everything, from woodland through to grassland, or devote the whole space to just one particular habitat, such as a perennial meadow, small copse or water garden. There is no prescriptive formula that renders one approach better than another, as long as you keep wildlife in mind.

Look too at the diversity of features and plants in the matrix of gardens that surrounds yours. Some of your neighbours' gardens will be laid mostly to lawn, others planted with fruit trees, herbaceous perennials and shrubs, while some may have a pond or even be derelict. All collectively have value. By clothing boundaries in climbers and linking trees and large shrubs on your side of the fence to those next door, you will also give the impression that your garden is larger than it is, as well as providing continuity of habitat and helping to strengthen corridors for wildlife through the urban sprawl.

RIGHT Formality meets naturalism in this contemporary woodland garden. Beneath the canopy of white-stemmed birch, a regiment of clipped box globes (*Buxus*) mingle with the bronze-tinted fern *Dryopteris erythrosora*, white Japanese anemone, *Anemone* x *hybrida* 'Honorine Jobert', red heucheras and the deciduous grass, *Hakonechloa macra* 'All Gold'. These and other plants provide cover for wildlife throughout the year.

squeezing wildlife into tiny spaces

WHILE OPTIONS FOR WILDLIFE GARDENING and naturalistic-style plantings are greater for large plots, it is perfectly possible to create similar features in confined spaces, such as courtyards and patios, or even on balconies and roof terraces. Many features can be scaled down and plants and wildflowers added to pots, containers, raised beds or temporary growing bags.

Seasonal pots

In small gardens, choose plants with long seasons of interest for container displays. Include those that bloom for months rather than weeks, as well as plants with interesting and useful seed heads that last through autumn or winter, such as annual poppies and love-in-a-mist (*Nigella*), perennial and annual grasses, and teasels. When the potted wildflowers have finished in midsummer, replace them with autumn-flowering salvias, zinnias or single-flowered dahlias to provide a late blast of colour and valuable nectar for bees.

If your terrace or courtyard is shaded, choose perennials, such as foxgloves, heucheras and ferns, that provide evocations of woodland plants, and spring bulbs, including snowdrops, crocus and dwarf daffodils, which offer early insect foragers much needed sustenance.

In hot, dry spaces, pot up hardy succulents, such as *Sedum* or *Crassula,* or mesembryanthemums like *Dorotheanthus,* which will be covered with gaudily coloured flowers when the sun shines. Late sedums, such as *S. spectabile* or *S. telephium,* have sculptural foliage and heads

OPPOSITE TOP A roof garden becomes an aerial meadow featuring a variety of ornamental grasses, including cultivars of *Miscanthus sinensis* and *Ampelodesmos mauritanicus,* drought-tolerant herbs, such as rosemary and fennel, and the tall pink perennial *Verbena bonariensis.*

OPPOSITE BOTTOM LEFT Even the smallest spaces can be planted for wildlife. Here a collection of moulded concrete planters contains a range of colourful, drought-tolerant succulent plants, such as houseleeks (*Sempervivum*) and sedums, which require very little care, save an occasional watering.

OPPOSITE BOTTOM RIGHT A casual and incidental atmosphere reigns in this relaxed arrangement of perennials in rustic stone planters set around a tiny decked terrace.

CLIMBING HIGH

Think about maximising use of your tiny space by clothing existing shrubs with smaller-scale climbers; *Clematis alpina* or *C. macropetala* or the smaller hybrids are ideal, or opt for annual climbers, such as sweetpeas. Wall space is another important resource for planting. Woody, self-clinging climbers, such as ivy (right) or climbing hydrangea, provide nesting and roosting sites for birds, while the heavenly scented flowers of honeysuckles offer a feast for butterflies, and attractive red berries in late summer and autumn for birds. Also consider installing a green wall planting system packed with a range of drought-tolerant plants to add value to your vertical spaces.

of nectar-rich flowers that will be besieged with bees and butterflies in late summer. With a little more moisture, many alpine plants, such as *Phlox subulata* and the dwarf hardy geraniums, *Geranium cinereum* and *G. subcaulescens,* will provide mats of spring and summer flowers in patio containers.

Grassy beds

Small borders or raised beds are ideal for clump-forming, non-invasive prairie grasses, such as the feathery *Stipa tenuissima* or taller *Stipa gigantea* with its oat-like flowers, upright purple moor grass (*Molinia*) or switch grass (*Panicum*). Summer flowers, such as *Echinacea, Salvia, Veronica* and geraniums, can be woven through the grasses to provide longer-term colour and seasonal interest. Annuals, including *Ammi majus,* yellow tidy-tips (*Layia platyglossa*) or love-in-a-mist (*Nigella damascena*) can also be sown into gaps or introduced as plugs.

Flowering roofs

Relatively flat roof space on a shed, garage or outbuilding could be converted into a green roof and covered with succulents or other drought-tolerant mat-forming species. Although the technology for creating green roofs has significantly advanced in recent years, it is always wise to consult a qualified, experienced installer or civil engineer before starting, to ensure your structure can withstand the weight of the installation and is appropriate for such a feature.

LEFT This skilfully designed roof garden meadow shades a contemporary arbour, which has been built to accommodate the weight of such a feature.

TOP RIGHT A vibrant pink form of *Phlox subulata* cascades over the edge of a raised bed.

CENTRE RIGHT A balcony vegetable garden sports tomatoes, brassicas and salad crops, together with pollinator-attracting buddleia and edible English marigolds, which both support many types of insect.

BELOW RIGHT The annual flower, love-in-a-mist, (*Nigella damascena*), is ideal for sowing between small shrubs, such as lavender, or non-invasive ornamental grasses.

> ❝ Even though many front gardens end up being used for parking cars, in most cases you can squeeze in areas of planting to make them more attractive to wildlife. ❞

ABOVE Use pots and containers to create a rolling display of plants from spring bulbs, herbs and shrubs to summer annuals, bringing life and colour to your front garden, which may also be used for parking the car.

OPPOSITE Allotments provide space for flowers as well as crops, and by planting wild or nectar-rich species, you can enliven the look of the plot while encouraging pollinators to visit. These vital insects will also help to pollinate fruiting crops, such as tomatoes, courgettes, and berries.

bringing wildlife into your community

OPPORTUNITIES TO USE WILDFLOWER and naturalistic plantings outside the confines of your back garden abound. Front gardens are an obvious area and often go unloved and unused, when they could be making a positive contribution to the environment and to wildlife. Even though many end up being used for parking cars, in most cases you can squeeze in areas of planting to make them more attractive to wildlife. An additional benefit of increasing the planting area in a front garden is that the soil and plants will absorb excess rainwater and reduce the risk of localised street flooding.

If there is no space for beds, use containers that have the requisite style or gravitas for your plantings. Pots, growing bags or upcycled containers can be planted with mixtures of colourful annuals or drought-tolerant perennials that will add interest for many months. Once annual flowering plants have faded, they can be removed and replaced with later-flowering species to continue the display.

Also adorn fences and walls with annual and perennial climbers – they take up little ground space and there are forms to suit gardens of all sizes and situations. If you have a small lawn in front of the house, try naturalising a few spring bulbs, such as snowdrops, crocuses or scillas, or if moist or shady, plant perennials, such as primroses (*Primula vulgaris*) or cowslips (*Primula veris*). Alternatively, stop worrying about maintaining perfect turf and accept those plants that may be thought of as weeds, such as daisies or speedwell – all benefit insects and you will no longer need to use weedkillers.

Blooming allotments

Allotments offer a wonderful stage set for wildflower mixtures and perennials, encouraging pollinators as well as making the place a little more vibrant. Some wildflowers can also be cut for indoor displays. Sow or plant a few on part of your plot or, with the cooperation of others, around the margins of the site or on plots that are not being tended.

You may also like to join a community gardening project in your area, many of which assume responsibility for neglected plots of public land. Collaborations such as these between public bodies and local residents are really valuable and offer a range of ways to directly influence the look of the local environment and increase wildflower and naturalistic plantings. Most community groups also use methods that are more in tune with nature, rather than installing traditional and often uninspiring bedding schemes that are both unsustainable and of little value to wildlife.

planning a wild garden

2

The growing conditions in this small garden are influenced by the hedge, which provides shelter but also shades the site for part of the day and draws moisture from the soil. Drought-tolerant sun-lovers, such as *Stachys* and *Verbascum,* are set where they receive the most light.

make your garden wild

To achieve your vision of a wild garden, it pays to first check your site and soil conditions and to also consider existing plants and features, working with nature to modify what you have, as well as adding new elements where they are needed.

Before you begin

When creating a wild garden, there are a few factors to consider first before choosing a type and style of planting. For example, while you may love the look of an annual wildflower meadow, its success depends on an open, sunny site and soil with low fertility. You also have to be prepared for one or two seasons when interest will be low. Take a look at these tips before making your final decision:

- **Marry site and style** Assess your soil conditions and aspect – the amount of light and moisture your garden receives – and match them with a wild landscape. This will ensure your chosen scheme will thrive in your garden. Sunny sites are perfect for meadows, Mediterranean-style schemes and many perennial plantings, while woodland and related understorey perennial plants suit shade.

- **Prepare the ground** Before planting, invest time in ensuring your soil is free of deep-rooted or pernicious perennial weeds, such as bindweed, field thistle and ground elder. It is far more difficult to remove them once plantings are in place, and while weeding may be time-consuming, your efforts will pay dividends. Also ensure your soil is prepared well for your chosen planting scheme (see also pp.46–47 and pp.50–51).

- **Assess seasons of interest** In large gardens, you can divide and screen areas that perform at different times of the year, but in a smaller space, which is on view at all times, a scheme with year-

TOP RIGHT A copse of young birch trees makes a dramatic feature in a small, damp meadow. This effect can be created by planting sapling trees, spacing them close together initially and then thinning out the weakest.

BOTTOM RIGHT Fruiting trees and shrubs are valuable additions to the wild garden, providing visual interest and valuable food for overwintering birds. Hawthorn (right), rowan, dogwood and elderberry are all worth including.

" Whether you opt to be completely organic or allow targeted use of pesticides and weedkillers, your choices will influence the approach and techniques you employ to create your wild garden. "

round interest would be preferable. This may mean devoting just a small area to annual wildflowers, which will look stunning while in flower but offer little interest at other times.

- **Consider the climate** Your garden's climate will determine the success (or failure) of various plantings. Drought, heavy rain and high winds can play havoc with delicate plants, particularly meadow flowers, so if your site is regularly affected by adverse weather, choose plants that are naturally resilient.

- **Reduce chemical usage** Whether you opt to be completely organic or allow targeted use of pesticides and weedkillers, your choices will influence the approach and techniques you employ to create your wild garden. If adopting an organic approach, you will need to accept that from time to time pests and diseases will affect your plants. What's more, it is nonsensical and damaging to the environment to use pesticides profligately when trying to encourage wildlife. Selecting disease-resistant varieties, choosing a style that best suits your circumstances and employing methods that maintain the health of your plants will help ward off many problems and spur you on the road to success.

TOP LEFT Meadow flowers suit sunny sites and free-draining, infertile soil. In shady areas, choose woodland species instead, and where soil is moist and fertile, try a bog garden.

BOTTOM LEFT Use plants that are best suited to conditions on your site, such

as these lavenders growing in well-drained soil beside a sunny terrace.

BELOW Avoid using fertilisers that may run off your beds and pollute ornamental and wild ponds or streams, and use harvested rainwater to replenish and refresh stagnant pools.

assessing your site

GARDENS CAN BE SEEN AS A CANVAS, and while the artist gardener may try to paint a picture that conveys their creative vision by imposing degrees of control over nature, it will relentlessly shift back to its natural state when left to its own devices. Assessment of your site is the most important part of the design process, and careful planning at the outset will enable you to choose plants and features that are adapted to your particular site.

Look at the context in which your garden sits and how it fits into the landscape. If you have a property in the country, are you surrounded by fields of crops or pastureland, or are there hedgerows that could link up with the garden? Perhaps you back on to woodland or have a natural stream nearby. In suburban gardens, check what features your neighbours have: do they have hedges or just fences, trees or water features? Look for clues like these to inspire ideas for your own plot and weave in neighbouring features, building on them in new, fresh and creative ways. For example, you could extend an existing hedgerow, divert a natural stream to make a wildlife pond, or add something new, such as a bog garden or small copse of trees. Water, shelter and cover for birds are among the most valuable elements you can bring to a garden, creating an aesthetic that pleases both you and the wildlife that visits it.

Make a plan

While any habitat will be of value, its size and scale is important too. They can determine whether or not planting schemes will be sustainable or need regular management, perhaps requiring you to supplement the plants every year or two. The long-term success of your schemes will also have a knock-on effect on wildlife, which may disappear if the plants they need are not available.

Try marshalling your garden features and design ideas onto a plan. Sketch a simple scale drawing of your site and, in ink, add permanent features, such as the house and boundaries. Also include existing plants, such as trees, shrubs, and perennials, that you wish to keep, marking the extent of the trees' canopies and whether they are evergreen or deciduous. Note, too, the orientation of the garden, showing the sunny and shady areas. Then, in pencil, sketch out your rough designs, with new beds, borders and planted spaces – pencil allows you to experiment and change your mind.

Your plan will highlight areas that will be difficult to plant up, such as dense shade cast by trees. One solution to this problem would be to raise or thin the canopies to let in more light and plant woodland or shade-tolerant species beneath. Alternatively, you could plan a small woodland by including more trees, or conversely clear a space to create sufficient light for a meadow.

BELOW TOP See changes in level as an opportunity to create drama and excitement in your design, and for making terraces for sitting or socialising.

BELOW BOTTOM Use the surrounding landscape to extend your garden space. Here, the trees beyond the garden boundary create a leafy backdrop to a sinuous water feature surrounded by lush planting.

❛ The type of soil, its acidity or alkalinity, the nutrients it holds – especially nitrogen and phosphorus – and its ability to hold moisture and drain, collectively influence the type of plants that will grow. ❜

getting down to earth

THE SITE AND SOIL CONDITIONS are the most important factors to take into account when formulating your plans for a wild garden. Not only do they directly determine what you can grow, but they also influence the way in which features and plants evolve over time. The type of soil, its acidity or alkalinity (known as its pH value), the nutrients it holds, especially nitrogen and phosphorus, and its ability to hold moisture and drain freely collectively influence the type of plants that will grow; even subtle variations can have a profound effect. New-build or brownfield sites may also include building rubble and a range of soils, producing a complex mix of conditions.

The way in which the ground slopes and undulates will affect plant growth too. High spots and areas at the top of a slope are much drier than those at the bottom, where water collects and promotes lush, more vigorous growth. Surrounding features, such as trees, which cast shade and dry the soil, are also influential, while buildings and fences may not only shade the garden but can prevent rainfall from reaching the ground, creating a rain shadow where many plants will struggle to survive.

TESTING YOUR SOIL'S TEXTURE, COMPOSITION & DRAINAGE

1. SOIL TEXTURE
As well as testing the soil in your garden for its acidity or alkalinity (see box opposite), also check if it is free-draining and sandy, rich in clay, or a mixture of both, known as 'loam'. To do this, take a soil sample, moisten it, and then roll it between your fingers. Soils with a high clay content will feel smooth and stick together to form a ball, while sandy soils will feel gritty and fall apart when rolled.

2. SOIL COMPOSITION
To accurately assess the quality and type of soil you have, dig pits at various points across your site and look at the soil profile (see above). Note the relative depth of the darker, nutrient-rich topsoil, and paler, nutrient-poor subsoil. The profile above is a heavy clay soil, with a thin layer of topsoil that is difficult to work, while the profile on the right is a well-drained loam, apt to drying out in summer.

3. THE WATER TABLE HEIGHT
While digging soil pits, check how well your soil drains too, as this will also affect your plant choices. If water fills the pit naturally in summer, you have a high water table; the area may flood in winter but would make an ideal spot for a natural pond or bog garden. If water fails to drain after a day or so, you may have heavy clay subsoil or an impervious layer that needs breaking up.

CHECKING SOIL ACIDITY

Before choosing your plants, test your soil's acidity, known as its pH value, using a soil test kit. This information is important as some plants will only thrive on acid soils, while others prefer more alkaline conditions.

Take a soil sample from just below the surface, and leave it to dry. Then follow the instructions on the kit, which normally require you to add a powder and testing solution to your sample. Compare the colour of the final solution with the chart supplied to identify whether your soil is acidic, neutral or alkaline. Test a few soil samples from a number of different sites around your garden, as the pH may not be the same throughout.

PLANT OPTIONS FOR DIFFERENT SOIL TYPES

(T – tree, S – shrub, P – perennial, G – grass)

PLANTS FOR SANDY DRY SOIL

- *Acanthus* (all) P
- *Betula* (all) T
- *Cercis* (all) T/S
- *Cotoneaster* (all) S
- *Echinops* (all) P
- *Euphorbia* (many) P
- *Festuca* (all) G
- *Genista* (all) S (pictured)
- *Hemerocallis* (all) P
- Iris - bearded (all) P
- *Miscanthus sinensis* G
- *Pinus* (all) T/S

PLANTS FOR HEAVY CLAY SOIL

- *Alchemilla mollis* P
- *Alnus* (all) T
- *Anemone x hybrida* P
- *Aster* (most) P
- *Astrantia* (all) P
- *Carpinus* (all) T
- *Cornus* (all) T/S
- *Kniphofia* (all) P
- *Mahonia* (all) S
- *Ribes* (all) S
- *Rosa* (all) S (pictured)
- *Viburnum* (all) S

PLANTS FOR ACID SOIL

- *Astilbe* (all) P
- *Amsonia* (all) P
- *Betula* (all) T
- *Calluna vulgaris* S
- *Erica carnea* S
- *Gaultheria* S
- *Kalmia* (all) S
- *Molinia caerulea* G
- *Persicaria* (all) P
- *Pieris* (all) S (pictured)
- *Primula* (many) P
- *Rhododendron* and azalea S

PLANTS FOR CHALKY ALKALINE SOIL

- *Achillea* (all) P
- *Carpinus* (all) T
- *Berberis* (all) S
- *Ceanothus* (all) S
- *Dianthus* (all) P
- *Geranium* (all) P
- *Helenium* (all) P
- *Lonicera* (all) S
- *Lavandula* (all) S
- *Salvia* (many) P, S (pictured)
- *Stipa gigantea* G
- *Syringa* (all) S

take a look at the sun

ASPECT, OR THE AMOUNT OF SUNLIGHT reaching the ground in your garden each day and cumulatively over the year, will influence your planting choices. For example, a south-facing garden receives significantly more sun than north-facing sites. This means a southerly aspect warms earlier in the year and cools down later, and it will also be significantly hotter during the growing seasons. As a result, plants here start into growth and then mature and flower earlier, often by a number of weeks, than those growing in north-facing gardens. Conversely, plants that need continual warmth and direct sun to flower may not perform reliably in gardens that face north, although they may produce more extensive foliage cover, since leaves are generally sustained for longer in cool, moist conditions.

To check your aspect, stand with your back to the main property so that you are looking out over the garden, and use a compass to see which direction it faces. Most gardens, even relatively small plots, will have some areas of sun and shade, although, as we have seen, north-facing sites will be the darkest, while east-facing gardens will receive the most light in the morning, and west-facing areas will be sunniest in the evening. Also take a few snapshots of the garden at different times of the day and during different seasons to plot where the sun falls. This will help you to plan in a range of different habitats, such as woodland or areas of wildflowers.

BELOW LEFT Plan the layout and planting of the garden by identifying areas of sun and shade, not only through the day, but also over the year. This open sunny site would be ideal for many flowering plants, but the soil may be prone to drying out quickly, a factor that would need to be considered when designing a scheme.

BELOW RIGHT Be prepared to adapt and change your plantings as trees and shrubs develop. What was once a sunny site may ultimately be in shade, and slower growing perennials may eventually oust short-lived ones.

consider the maintenance

BEFORE STARTING ANY GARDEN PROJECT, consider the effort and investment your chosen scheme requires. The preparation for any new project will demand considerable time and energy at the start, but while some may take more than a year to establish, others, such as naturalising bulbs in existing turf, require less time. For large schemes, such as meadows or ponds, consider employing a specialist to plant, sow or build the feature. Similarly, it is wise to employ qualified tree surgeons to remove or reduce tall trees.

No garden is ever maintenance-free and whether your wild garden is new or mature, it will require routine and more intensive periodic management. That said, features such as meadows are more demanding than, say, shrubs and perennials, although even these require less effort than a large lawn that needs mowing regularly.

LOW MAINTENANCE FEATURES

- naturalised bulbs in grassland
- woodland or plantings in shade
- massed perennial plantings
- established water features
- gravel gardens planted with drought-tolerant species

HIGH MAINTENANCE FEATURES

- containerised planting displays
- areas with large lawns to mow
- meadows planted with annual wildflowers
- topiary or large areas of formal or closely trimmed hedging

❛ Some horticultural techniques used for wild gardens differ from common practices, and you may also need to make preparations a few weeks before planting or sowing. ❜

CREATING A SEEDBED

Create a seedbed in late summer for autumn sowing, or late winter for spring sowing. Seeds need a fine soil structure to obtain moisture and oxygen for germination. Fill in depressions in the bed and crush soil clods with the back of a rake. When sowing, the ground should be firm, but not compacted. To firm, shuffle along the surface with your feet, then rake to form a fine crumbly texture (tilth). In small plots reduce competition from weed seeds by covering the soil with a 2.5cm (1in) layer of washed horticultural sand, loam or peat-free seed compost and sow onto this.

preparing the ground

ENSURING THE GROUND IS WELL PREPARED is one of the most important aspects of wild gardening. It pays dividends to invest time in removing weeds and ensuring the soil is of the appropriate fertility and has the right structure for seed sowing or planting. Some techniques used for wild gardens differ from common horticultural practices, and you may also need to make preparations a few weeks before planting or sowing. The following tips offer a guide.

Making a border

Border shape, depth and location play a significant role in the success of a planting scheme. Fluid, sinuous shapes suit naturalistic designs and borders should be no less than 1.8m (6ft) deep. This will enable you to grow a wide range of plants, while achieving height, structure and impact.

- Dig the border before planting, removing weeds (see right) and breaking up compacted areas. Work the soil when it is dry and crumbly, and avoid using rotary cultivators if you can.
- Choosing plants that suit your soil conditions should reduce the need for soil improvement, but digging in well-rotted organic matter or compost will help improve the drainage in heavy clay soils and the water-holding ability of sandy soils that dry quickly.

WEEDING TECHNIQUES

Controlling rampant weed growth is one of the most critical factors in establishing any type of planting scheme, especially sown meadows, where it is far more difficult to intervene and remove weeds at a later stage. It is important to clear weeds from the planting area because they compete with ornamentals and wildflowers for light, water and nutrients, and some also carry diseases.

Established weeds, either perennials such as nettles and couch grass, or fast-growing shrubs, including elder, are more difficult to treat than annuals, and must be tackled in advance, using the methods outlined here, before you begin planting or sowing seed.

The existing bank of weed seeds in the soil will constantly replenish annual and perennial species, and while some might be useful for pollinators, it is impossible to differentiate between these and more pernicious types, and so it is best to treat the lot.

Try the following methods to remove any unwanted weeds from your site.

COVERING THE GROUND

Blanketing the ground with an impervious barrier to exclude light is an unsightly, but effective method of killing annual and some perennial weeds. Materials to use include old carpet and black polythene, placed in position some months before the plot is required. Ideally, perennial weeds should be removed or controlled beforehand as they can persist by using stored food reserves in their roots. Barriers buy time for sowing or planting before more weed seeds are introduced on the wind or by birds and animals.

WEEDING BY HAND

It is essential to remove all the roots of pernicious perennial weeds, such as couch grass, bindweed, field thistle and nettles, to prevent their regeneration and further infestation. Nettles are the easiest to remove, as their root system grows in the upper soil layer, while deeply anchored, fragile-rooted species, such as bindweed and field thistle, need careful removal with a fork.

Tackle annual weeds with a hoe before sowing meadows, and as they appear between perennial plants and shrubs.

USING CHEMICAL CONTROLS

Herbicides or weedkillers offer an effective way of removing weeds but try to limit their use in wild gardens. Perennial weeds need a translocated herbicide, such as glyphosate, which is absorbed into the plant tissues, killing the top growth and roots. Some species may need further applications. While glyphosate is also useful for annual weeds, other contact herbicides are available, including those made from natural oils. Always spray weedkillers on a still day, or spot treat problem weeds with aerosol or dab-on applicators. And always follow the manufacturer's instructions.

MULCHING

A mulch is a thick layer of a material, such as bark chips, crushed stone, composted waste or gravel, that limits the light needed for weed seed germination. Mulches are applied after the ground has been cleared of perennial weeds and usually after planting. Use them to cover the whole surface or spot-place a mulch around each plant. Besides controlling annual weeds, mulches help conserve moisture and regulate soil temperature. To be effective, they should be at least 5cm (2in) deep and will need to be replaced periodically as they are scattered by wind or wildlife, or deteriorate.

basic planting tips

SUCCESSFUL PLANTING is all about adequate preparation and using healthy plants or seed mixes suited to your garden conditions. Prepare the ground in advance and remove weeds (see pp.50–51). Planting times also exert a profound effect, and while spring is traditionally seen as the right time, late-summer and autumn are often better for many plants, as the soil is still warm, encouraging root growth and the establishment of hardy seedlings, so they get off to a faster start in spring.

Avoid plants that have been in pots too long as this may inhibit their growth – check that there are no long or tangled roots growing through the drainage holes. Woody plants in particular suffer if they have been pot bound and may die after planting. Once in, plants will need watering in dry weather until well established.

BIODEGRADABLE POTS

When sown in biodegradable pots, half-hardy annual and perennial seedlings can be planted directly into the ground, pot and all. If no roots appear to be growing through the pot wall at planting time gently tear the sides first.

SOWING MEADOW MIXES

Sowing seeds to create floral meadows is a spectacular, fast and cost-effective way of bringing naturalistic style to your garden. While blithely scattering the contents of any seed pack will result in some form of display, taking more care will help ensure the results are more successful. Choose a mixture suited to your conditions – most seed suppliers provide helpful advice about this – and create a clean seedbed, as free from competition from other weed seedlings as possible (see pp.50–51). Seeds can be sown at any time of year, but the best time is spring, when increasing temperatures and high soil moisture levels promote quick germination and the resulting seedlings establish large root systems. Hardy meadow seeds can sometimes be sown in autumn (check with suppliers), overwintering as seedlings and mimicking what happens in nature. Follow these tips for sowing a small patch of meadow seed.

1 MAKE A WEED-FREE BED
Remove perennial weeds. Then make a small, weed-free seedbed by spreading a 2.5cm (1in) layer of washed horticultural sand or sterilised seed compost onto the soil surface.

2 SOWING SEEDS EVENLY
Sow evenly and densely enough so that your plants out-compete native weed species. Some meadow seed mixes are formulated to germinate quickly to help achieve this.

3 THIN THE SEEDLINGS
In small areas, if you want to achieve a balanced mix of flowers, thin plants accordingly, but only if you can confidently identify the flower seedlings. One idea is to take pictures of the seedlings as they grow, enabling you to recognise them the following year.

SOWING ANNUALS IN TRAYS AND POTS

Growing your own annual or perennial flowers and grasses from seed is a very satisfying part of the wild gardening process. A wide range of home-grown plants, such as cosmos (above) can be raised in modules or small plastic pots, and when grown in a protected environment, such as a greenhouse, coldframe or on a windowsill indoors, success rates are generally higher than for seed sown in situ outside. Modules come in various sizes, from tiny 2.5cm (1in) plugs, through to 7cm (3in) cell trays – the latter are good for all tasks, enabling seed sowing through to growing on individual perennials or clumps of annual seedlings. You will also require sufficient space to store all the young plants until they are large enough to plant out, so do moderate your ambitions!

❶ SOWING SEED IN MODULES

Fill the cells in the tray with moist seed compost and firm with a tamper or piece of plywood to create a level surface. Sow seed evenly over the compost and cover as instructed. Keep moist until seeds germinate.

❸ POSITION IN EVEN LIGHT

Set your seedlings in a greenhouse or, if hardy, in a coldframe. You can put them on a windowsill indoors, but remember to turn them every day or two to prevent them growing tall and spindly (etiolated) and stretching towards the light.

❺ GROWING ON

Gradually increase the outdoor exposure over a two-week period, until the seedlings are outside all day. You can then plant out hardy types, but delay planting half-hardy plants until after the frosts.

❷ PRICKING OUT

Once seedlings are large enough to handle, carefully remove each one, or small clumps of three seedlings, and plant them in individual modules or 9cm (3½in) pots of seed and cutting compost.

❹ HARDENING OFF

When the seedlings' roots start growing through the drainage holes in the modules or pots, acclimatise them to lower outdoor temperatures (known as 'hardening off'). Place them in a coldframe or outside for a few hours during the day, and bring them back inside at night.

❻ PLANTING OUT

Moisten root balls before planting, and loosen soil in the planting holes. Firm plants in position and water in. Keep watered until plants are established, and protect young plants from slugs and snails.

PLANTING CLIMBERS AND WALL SHRUBS

Climbers and shrubs on walls and fences adds to a site's wildlife habitats. How your chosen plants clamber up (see right) determines the type of support they require, but all climbers and wall shrubs are planted in the same way. Pot-grown plants can be planted at any time of year, while bare-root types must be planted while dormant in winter. Position the climber or shrub at least 30cm (12in) away from the surface it is to cover, and tie the stems to canes slanted towards the wall or structure.

SELF-CLINGING CLIMBERS

Campsis, ivy (*Hedera*) and *Hydrangea petiolaris* produce small stem roots that adhere to walls or tree trunks. *Parthenocissus* has tendrils with sticky disks that do likewise.

Supports needed

To root, stems must be in contact with the surface they are to climb. Hold them in position temporarily with a wooden plank or tile. *Parthenocissus* will climb spontaneously.

Climbers for wildlife
- *Campsis radicans*
- *Hedera* species
- *Hydrangea anomola* subsp. *petiolaris*
- *Parthenocissus* species
- *Schizophragma*
- *Trachelospermum*

TENDRIL CLIMBERS

Plants such as *Cobaea*, *Lathyrus* and *Vitis* produce outgrowths of leaves or stems which clasp supports. Clematis has twining leaf-stalks.

Supports needed

Provide supports on which plants can clamber, such as trellis, plastic mesh or adjacent shrubs. Many can also be grown on obelisks or other ornamental features.

Climbers for wildlife
- *Clematis* (most species)
- *Cobaea* species
- *Eccremocarpus scaber*
- *Lathyrus* (many species)
- *Passiflora* species
- *Vitis* (most species)

TWINING CLIMBERS

Stems twine tightly around supports or other plants and the shoots then harden. Vigorous species, such as *Wisteria*, need sturdy supports, such as heavy duty wires fixed to walls.

Supports needed

Provide supports that match the robustness of the plants. These can be canes, trellis, timber and sturdy wire frames. Tie shoots in until plants start to twine on their own.

Climbers for wildlife
- *Actinidia* species
- *Akebia* species
- *Jasminum* (many species)
- *Lonicera* (many species)
- *Schisandra* species
- *Wisteria* species

PLANTING PERENNIALS

The mainstay of many naturalistic schemes, perennials are usually bought as pot-grown specimens, although buying them as young plants or plugs will reduce the cost of planting large areas. Plan the size and spread of your chosen perennials beforehand, as this will determine how far apart they must be planted; large, vigorous perennials can be set further apart, since they will soon spread, while slower-growing or ground-cover types can be planted more densely.

- Before planting, water the plants in their pots. Dig a hole large enough to easily accommodate the root ball, and loosen the soil at the bottom of the hole with a fork.
- Most perennials are planted so that the top of the root ball is in line with the soil surface. Once the plants are in, firm the soil around them to remove any large air gaps. Water in well, and continue to water regularly until plants are well established.

PLANTING BULBS

Bulbs are easy and rewarding plants to grow in a wild garden. You can choose from a range of different types to provide splashes of colour for most of the year, but the majority flower in spring when they offer early sources of pollen and nectar for insects. Most bulbs, including snowdrops, narcissi, crocuses, tulips, muscari, and alliums, are planted in autumn, and flower in spring and early summer. Summer-flowering bulbs, such as lilies, cannas and dahlias, should be planted in the spring.

- Plant bulbs with their nose end at a depth of twice the height of the bulb; plant tulips a little deeper. When planting, ensure the pointed tip of the bulb is uppermost.
- For a natural effect, scatter the bulbs where needed and plant them where they fall. Use a bulb planter, or a narrow pointed trowel to plant bulbs individually or dig out an area to plant them en masse.
- There is no need to add fertiliser or water them in; the soil moisture will be sufficient.

❛ Although container-grown trees can, in theory, be planted at any time, autumn or late winter are best, allowing the roots to establish before the summer droughts arrive. ❜

ROOT BOOSTS

Some beneficial fungi (mycorrhizae) have a symbiotic relationship with plants' roots, and allow trees, shrubs and other plants to forage more effectively for water and nutrients. To give your plants a boost, add products containing these fungal spores to the soil in the planting hole.

planting trees and shrubs

YOU CAN BUY DECIDUOUS TREES as pot-grown, root-balled (roots and soil encased in a meshed fabric) or bare-root specimens. Evergreen trees and shrubs are almost always sold as pot-grown specimens in containers. Bare-root and root-balled trees should only be planted from late autumn to late winter when plants are dormant and the ground is not frozen. Although container-grown trees can, in theory, be planted at any time, autumn or late winter are best, allowing the roots to establish before the summer droughts arrive.

If considering a large specimen tree, ask your grower or specialist if you can visit the nursery to pick out your trees individually. Check that the top growth is healthy and, if possible, inspect the roots to ensure they are not too congested, which could suggest the tree has been containerised for too long and may not thrive after planting. Bare-root and root-balled trees should have a strong root system with both structural and finer feeding roots.

The planting advice for shrubs is the same as that for trees (opposite), except few shrubs will require staking.

TIPS FOR TREE (AND SHRUB) PLANTING

If trees and shrubs are to realise their full potential they need planting with care, since the method used can affect their establishment and subsequent growth. Most trees like moisture, but hate being waterlogged for any length of time. Roots and root hairs also develop and function more efficiently in well-aerated soil, rather than in dense, compacted conditions. Wet soils cause root rots and encourage diseases such as *Phytophthora*, a particularly devastating disease for conifers. If your soil is damp, choose a tree more suited to these conditions, such as *Alnus* species, *Betula pendula*, *Salix* species and *Sorbus aucuparia*, or plant on a mound of earth raised 15cm (6in) above ground level. Alternatively, install a drainage system. Also keep the area around a newly planted tree free from plants that will compete for water and nutrients, and use a tree guard if deer or rabbits are a problem.

❶ PREPARING TO PLANT

Before planting, improve the soil in the area by adding well-rotted organic matter to well-drained soils or grit to heavy clay. Dig the hole, preferably square, 45–60cm (18–24in) wider and the same depth as the tree's root ball. Fork over the bottom and sides of the hole to improve drainage. In heavy clay soils lever the sides with a fork to reduce compaction. On permanently wet soils, create a mound 15cm (6in) high and 1.2m (4ft) in diameter, and make a planting hole for the tree in the mound.

❷ IMPROVING CONDITIONS

Add slow-release fertiliser, such as bone meal or blood, fish and bone, at the recommended rate to the planting hole. You can also mix in preparations containing beneficial mycorrhizal fungi if you wish (see opposite), but always follow manufacturer's instructions with regard to application rates and use of additional fertilisers. Place the tree, still in its pot, into the hole to check the planting level.

❸ POSITION THE TREE

Ensure the top of the root ball is level with the soil surface, adding or removing the soil in the hole accordingly. Never bury the root ball too deeply in the soil, which may result in poor growth. Spread out the roots of bare and root-balled trees and cut out any that are damaged. Remove the pot of container-grown trees, tease out some of the roots, and position in the hole. Backfill with soil, firming gently to remove air pockets.

❹ STAKING AND AFTERCARE

After planting soak the root zone, and water well during dry or windy weather for the first year. Large or top-heavy trees will require staking. Drive in a tree stake about 10cm (4in) from the trunk, avoiding the roots, on the side of the prevailing wind. Attach using adjustable tree ties that can be loosened over time. Suppress weeds and help retain moisture by mulching the surface with a 7cm (3in) layer of bark chips.

creating meadow effects

3

The vivid, clashing tones of this annual meadow create a dramatic spectacle in early summer. Although many plants will naturally self-sow, the consistency of the effects are difficult to predict. If this is critical, small areas are best re-sown each year using fresh blends of seed.

meadows for gardens

❛ Different types of meadow require various levels of care. The frequency and timing of sowing, weeding, trimming and replanting should all be taken into consideration when making your selection. ❜

Whether recreating a slice of a traditional hayfield dotted with annual flowers or a perennial meadow made up of long-flowering species, the key to success is to match your site and soil conditions with the landscapes you wish to reflect.

Choosing a meadow type

Meadows and grasslands provide rich habitats for wildlife and produce breathtaking features in gardens large and small. Wild landscapes can provide the templates for our designs at home, and among the most potent are chalk grasslands – found in the UK in the South Downs and Derbyshire Peak District – and moist, flower-rich meadows. Hay meadows, now scarce in the countryside, can also offer inspiration. Garden designers have been influenced by grasslands worldwide, too, their ideas sourced from alpine meadows in Europe and Asia, dry herb-rich grassland of the Mediterranean maquis, the shrubby chaparral of California, and the iconic tall and short-grass prairies of North America's Southern states and Midwest.

The trick to recreating a meadow is to take the visual qualities of these natural, semi-natural or agricultural landscapes and translate their diversity of species, colour palettes and structure into scaled-down versions appropriate to your garden site and soil conditions.

Different types of meadow also require various levels of care. The frequency and timing of sowing, weeding, trimming and replanting should all be taken into consideration when making your selection. The following pages offer a detailed guide to the installation and care of a range of meadow types to help you choose.

BELOW A grassy meadow with naturalised quamash (*Camassia*) is a captivating sight in spring and easy to create. There are many other types of bulb that can be naturalised in grassland of different heights and for areas in full sun or partial shade.

sowing meadow mixes

OPPOSITE TOP Annual cornflowers (*Centaurea cyanus*) are available in a wide range of colours, from blue, through to pink, purple and white.

OPPOSITE BOTTOM An enchanting jewel-box of flowers from an annual blend shows what is possible from a successful broadcast sowing of seed.

BELOW The classic meadow planting of annual scarlet field poppies, blue cornflowers and white ox- eye daisies is a dramatic sight as summer peaks and it is easy to create from ready-blended seed mixtures.

MEADOWS CAN BE CREATED from mixtures of annual flowers, which grow, bloom and set seed in one year, or from perennials that flower in their first year and then bloom again over the following few years. Alternatively, you can opt for grasses and perennial wildflower mixtures or easy planting solutions, such as ready-to-use impregnated seed papers, or mats or turves of meadow plants that contain various blends of perennials and, in some cases, grass species.

Sowing annual mixes is one of the easiest and most rewarding ways of establishing a meadow effect, as the results are quick and colourful. They are really useful in small gardens that have areas of open ground, such as alongside a pathway, or gaps in borders, or you can use them in large pots. While most annual mixes require full sun, there are blends suitable for light shade, but not for deep shade. Some mixtures comprise a wide range of species, others recreate hay meadows and include scarlet poppies, blue and red flax, azure cornflowers, and pink or white corncockle. Alternatively, you can choose colour-themed blends in yellow, blue, pink, red or white.

FACTORS TO CONSIDER BEFORE SOWING ANNUALS

Ideal for:
- Small spaces
- Gaps in borders
- Hedgerow margins
- Containers

Advantages
- Cheap to create
- Easy to sow
- Fast establishment
- Flowers weeks from sowing

Disadvantages
- Weeds can dominate if seed is not sown correctly
- Sowing needs to be even for best results
- Flowering can be short or curtailed in poor weather
- Can look untidy after flowering season is over
- Ground looks untidy or bare out of season
- Areas may require re-sowing to maintain the flower display in successive years

SOWING ANNUAL FLOWER SEED

Quick and easy, this sowing method is ideal for the beginner who wants colourful annual flowers for a pathway, border or small meadow.

SITE: Full sun
SOIL: Free-draining
MAINTENANCE NEEDED: Medium

YOU WILL NEED

- Seed mixtures of choice
- Rake
- Loam-based or peat-free seed compost
- Garden sieve
- Watering can or hose

PLANT CHOICES

Meadow mixes available for:
- Bees, butterflies and other pollinators
- Woodland edge and shade-loving plants
- Colourful meadows
- Colour-themed meadow effects
- Various soil conditions
- Wild bird seed

1 PREPARE TO PLANT

In spring or late summer prepare a fine seedbed by levelling and firming the soil surface with a rake, breaking up any clods of earth. Ensure the soil surface is cleared of all perennial and established weed seedlings (see also p.51 for bed preparation).

2 SOW SEED EVENLY

Sow seed evenly, following the instructions on the packet. Some mixes come in a carton (above) to make sowing easier. You can also mix loose seed with dry, silver sand to help distribute the seeds evenly; it also identifies the sown areas.

3 THE COVER-UP

Lightly cover the sown area with sieved loam or peat-free seed compost, rather than garden soil which may contain weed seeds. Sowing on silver sand or seed compost will also help suppress weeds (see p.50).

4 SEEDLING CARE

Soak the area thoroughly with a can fitted with a fine rose head. Keep the soil moist during prolonged dry spells. For small areas, cover the bed with sweet pea netting to prevent birds eating the seeds (see p.68).

⑤ WATCH OUT FOR WEEDS

Allow seedlings to grow naturally, watering the bed only if the soil is very dry. Keep a watch for obvious vigorous weed seedlings such as nettles that could disrupt plantings and remove them carefully by hand.

⑥ AFTERCARE

Do not be tempted to apply liquid fertilisers, as they stimulate lush growth, causing the plants to collapse and reducing the flower display. If rain batters down the plants, shake off the excess and right the growth as carefully as possible. Unless you need seeds for birds, or you want plants to self-sow, remove them after flowering and re-sow the area again the following year. Some annuals will self-seed if left untouched until early autumn, but remember that the subsequent blend of plants will be unpredictable.

RIGHT Spangled with annual wildflowers, a neglected path-edging is transformed into a colourful miniature meadow.

WILDLIFE BENEFITS

- Food for the larvae of some beneficial insects
- Food for pollinating insects from early summer
- Seeds for birds and wildlife in autumn if plants left in situ

GROWING TIPS

- Clean the sowing area of all weeds beforehand
- Displays work best in nutrient poor soil, so do not add fertiliser
- Water until seedlings establish, and then only in dry conditions

USING SEED-IMPREGNATED PAPERS

Very easy to use and ideal for beginners or children, choose a paper appropriate to your needs and conditions, and let the display commence!

SITE: Full sun
SOIL: Free-draining
MAINTENANCE NEEDED: Low

YOU WILL NEED

- Impregnated seed paper or mat
- Rake to level site
- Loam-based or peat-free seed compost
- Garden sieve
- Watering can or hose

Paper and mat choices:
- Plants for bees and butterflies
- Cottage garden mixtures
- American wildflower mixtures
- Colour-themed plants, such as the blue mix of cornflowers, *Convolvulus* and *Phacelia*, shown here

❶ POSITION THE PAPER OR MAT

Prepare the soil in open ground in advance (see p.50), or use a raised bed, tub or half-barrel. Soak the ground using a hose or can with a fine spray. Position the paper or mat and cut to shape. Use excess in beds or pots.

❷ COVER WITH COMPOST

Weight down the paper or mat with stones or compost to keep it in position, particularly if windy. Also cover the mat with sieved loam-based or peat-free seed compost until it is just obscured.

❸ WATER UNTIL ESTABLISHED

Soak the paper or mat with a fine spray to prevent disturbing the soil. Replace the compost if areas of paper are revealed. Seeds will start to germinate in 7–10 days. Keep moist until seedlings are established.

❹ FLOWER CARE

As the seedlings develop, the paper soon rots away. Remove any weed seedlings as they appear. You may need to thin vigorous plants, but these products generally do not require further care apart from watering.

HARVEST YOUR SEEDS

Seed from your own plants is very easy to collect, and many plants, particularly hardy annuals, biennials and short-lived perennials, produce copious amounts which you can use to regenerate them. Leave plants for a few weeks after flowering to allow the seed to set, and harvest when the pods have just turned brown before splitting. Place the pods in a labelled paper envelope, either in a mix or as separate species. Store in a cool, dry place until the seeds have shed. Remove any remaining seeds from the husks and transfer them all to a new, labelled envelope. Again, keep them in a cool, dry place until required.

WILDLIFE BENEFITS

- Food for insect larvae and pollinating insects
- Food for birds and wildlife in autumn

GROWING TIPS

- Remove weeds before laying papers and as they appear in the summer
- Nutrient poor soil is best, so do not add any fertilisers
- Water until seedlings establish, then water only in dry conditions

SOWING FLOWER SEED IN SHADE

In areas that receive just a few hours of sun each day, choose a seed mix of shade-tolerant annuals, biennials and perennials.

SITE : Part shade
SOIL: Moist, free-draining
MAINTENANCE NEEDED: Medium

YOU WILL NEED

- Seed mixtures of choice
- Rake to level site
- Bag of loam-based, peat-free compost or silver sand
- Watering can or hose

PLANT CHOICES

Plants available in shade-tolerant meadow mixes:
- *Agrimonia eupatoria*
- *Campanula trachelium*
- *Digitalis purpurea*
- *Myosotis sylvatica*
- *Myrrhis odorata*
- *Primula vulgaris*
- *Prunella vulgaris*
- *Silene dioica*
- *Stachys officinalis* (above)
- *Teucrium scorodonia*

❶ MAKE A STERILE SEEDBED

Prepare an even and fine seedbed (see p.50). Alternatively, sow onto a sterile surface, which suppresses weed seeds. To do this, lay 1cm (½in) of silver sand, seed compost or subsoil, and sow at the recommended rates.

❸ PROTECT FROM BIRDS

Birds, such as pigeons, can cause problems by scratching around for seeds. To prevent this damage, cover small areas with sweet pea netting or use deterrents such as tin-foil plates or foil strips on canes.

❷ COVER AND WATER

If instructed on the pack, cover the seed with a fine layer of sieved seed compost. Water with a can fitted with a fine rose and keep the bed moist. Seeds sown in shade are slower to germinate and establish than those in sun.

❹ SLOW GERMINATION

Until the seedlings have a few leaves, keep them watered in dry weather. Germination may be patchy in shadier areas and you may need to re-sow. Remove any protective netting when plants are established.

ABOVE A naturalistic grouping of cow parsley, red campion, forget-me-not and *Camassia* bulbs, which all luxuriate in moist, semi-shaded conditions, as well as in sun, in early summer. This mix of early summer flowers also supplies a rich food source for pollinating insects.

WILDLIFE BENEFITS

- Food for the larvae of some beneficial insects
- Food for pollinating insects from early summer
- Seeds for birds and wildlife in autumn if plants left in situ

GROWING TIPS

- Clear the sowing area of all weeds beforehand
- Displays work best in nutrient poor soil, so do not add fertiliser
- Water until seedlings establish, then only in dry conditions

sowing grass and wildflower mixes

GRASSY MEADOWS DOTTED WITH WILDFLOWERS is something many gardeners aspire to, and there are seed blends to suit a wide range of site conditions. Many specialist suppliers offer an advice service to help you select the best mixes for your conditions, but check your soil's pH and make-up first (see p.47), as this will affect your options. If you're planning to sow a large area, you may wish to commission a specialist company to do this, as they have the knowledge, experience and equipment to undertake such work.

Sowing a small area with a meadow blend is no different to sowing any wildflower mix and the same techniques apply. Prepare the site (see p.50) and sow seed in autumn or spring when the ground is moist, yet still firm enough to walk on. Cutting the meadow must be timed accurately to ensure plants shed their seed to promote next year's display; the supplier should include advice on when to do this, but it is normally in midsummer. Always remove and compost the grass clippings to prevent them smothering the flower seedlings below and also, through decomposition, increasing the soil's fertility. Never apply fertilisers unless the supplier recommends it, as this will encourage rampant grass growth rather than flowers.

If your soil is too rich, you can help to remedy the problem by inverting the topsoil with less fertile subsoil, so the subsoil is at the surface; you then sow on that (see p.75 for instructions). You can also plant yellow rattle, *Rhinanthus minor*, which is partially parasitic and helps to keep the grasses in check (see box opposite).

FACTORS TO CONSIDER BEFORE SOWING GRASS AND WILDFLOWER MIXES

Ideal for:
- Areas in sun or semi-shade
- Gardens of any size
- Sloping sites
- Rough ground

Advantages
- Relatively cheap to establish meadows
- Mixtures can be tailored for different sites
- Grass component provides cover in winter
- Can take some foot traffic

Disadvantages
- Poor weather after sowing can affect establishment of some wildflower species
- Rich soils will boost the growth of vigorous grasses, squeezing out the less vigorous wildflowers
- Correct maintenance is essential if grasses are not to overwhelm less vigorous wildflowers

SOWING WILDFLOWERS WITH GRASSES

SITE: Full sun or part sun
SOIL: Free-draining
MAINTENANCE NEEDED: Medium

YOU WILL NEED
- Seed mixtures of choice
- Rake and spade
- Watering can or hose
- Manual rotary or sit-on mower

PLANT CHOICES

Meadow mixes available:
- For various soil conditions
- Woodland edge and shaded areas
- Bees, butterflies and other pollinators
- Native species mixtures
- Low grassland/turf mixtures

WILDLIFE BENEFITS

- Food for pollinating insects
- Seeds for birds and wildlife in autumn
- Habitat and food for insect and invertebrate larvae
- Habitat for amphibians and larger wildlife

GROWING TIPS

- Marry meadow mix to soil conditions
- Prepare the site well and remove perennial weeds
- Water meadow in first year in prolonged dry periods
- Mow as advised on seed pack and remove clippings

INCREASING FLOWER DIVERSITY WITH YELLOW RATTLE

Rhinanthus minor, or yellow rattle, is a native annual meadow plant. Partially parasitic, it obtains some nutrients from grass, which reduces the grasses' vigour, enabling other flowering plants to thrive. It can be sown in existing grasslands and should be introduced before wildflowers.

BELOW When properly managed and maintained, a grassy wildflower meadow is an object of beauty, both in its entirety and in close proximity as the plant communities change and develop throughout the year.

1 MARRY SITE WITH SEED CHOICE

Prepare the site thoroughly beforehand, removing perennial weeds by hand or with herbicides. Evaluate your soil, testing the pH to identify if it's acid or alkaline, sandy, chalky or heavy clay (see p.47–48). Select a meadow mix suitable for your conditions. Sow at rates recommended by the manufacturer, preferably in the autumn to allow all the plants to germinate before spring.

2 KEEP MOWING

Water the young plants in the first year, and mow the meadow to 15cm (6in) in height in late spring. Mow again at the same height, in midsummer and then again anytime between late autumn and late winter. After each mowing, remove the clippings to reduce the grasses' vigour. Remove any perennial weeds too. The meadow will start to flower properly in the second year.

3 MEADOW AFTERCARE

To maintain the diversity of flowers in your grassland year after year, always follow the seed supplier's instructions and only cut the meadow after plants have shed their seed. Remove the clippings after cutting and never apply fertilisers or mulches, which will encourage rampant grass growth at the expense of flowers. You can over-seed with yellow rattle and other wildflowers to boost the meadow's diversity (see box above).

sowing perennial mixtures

SOWING A RANGE OF PERENNIALS offers a more permanent solution to establishing attractive plant communities. They usually comprise biennials and short-lived perennials, such as foxgloves and *Verbascum*, which survive for just a few years, as well as more reliably perennial species, including *Centaurea*, *Rudbeckia* and *Sanguisorba*. Many will flower in their first year if sown early enough, either in the autumn or late winter when the ground is not waterlogged or frozen.

Sowing is just as easy as that for annuals, but always follow the supplier's instructions. The floral effects are often less exuberant than you would achieve with annual mixes, but the benefit is that for the most part you sow just once to achieve long-lasting meadow effects. However, do take into account that the shorter-lived plants, such as foxgloves (*Digitalis*), *Verbascum* and *Coreopsis* will need to self-seed back into gaps between the other plants after flowering to ensure a future display; you can help to encourage this by scattering a few seeds here and there in late summer or autumn.

After a few years, some of the perennials that thrive in your conditions may start to dominate at the expense of others, but once established you can thin these out while supplementing other species to change the look or extend the season of interest. After the plants have flowered, remove spent flower heads to tidy up the display and encourage further blooms to form; alternatively leave them to seed until early spring and then cut stems down before new shoots appear.

❛ The floral effects of perennials are often less exuberant than you would achieve with annual mixes, but the benefit is that for the most part you sow once to achieve long-lasting effects. ❜

LEFT A perennial meadow sown with *Echinacea*, *Rudbeckia* and *Coreopsis* bursts into bloom in high summer.

ABOVE Slim, long-flowering plants, such as *Coreopsis verticillata*, are used in many perennial meadow mixes and make good partners for other blooms.

FACTORS TO CONSIDER BEFORE SOWING PERENNIALS

Ideal for:
- Small to medium-sized garden spaces
- Adding to new and existing herbaceous perennial and shrub plantings

Advantages
- Cheap to produce long-lasting effects
- Easy to sow
- More permanent and weather-resistant than an annual meadow
- Longer season of interest than with annuals
- Covers the ground for longer periods, especially in winter
- Can be adapted by adding your own perennials later

Disadvantages
- Needs to be sown evenly for the best effects
- Flower range is more limited
- Poor weather can affect establishment
- Weed control needed
- Plant community can change from year to year

SOWING PERENNIAL MEADOW PLANTS

Perennial plants may take longer than annuals to germinate and establish, but they make up for this by flowering year after year.

SITE: Full sun or part shade
SOIL: Any soil, but not wet
MAINTENANCE NEEDED: Medium

YOU WILL NEED

- Perennial seed mixes of choice
- Seed and potting compost
- Seed and cell trays, pots
- Sowing tools
- Watering can with fine rose attachment

PLANT CHOICES

Perennial mixes include
- *Achillea filipendulina*
- *Centaurea scabiosa*
- *Coreopsis lanceolata*
- *Digitalis* species
- *Echinacea purpurea*
- *Knautia arvensis*
- *Leucanthemum vulgare*
- *Malva moschata*
- *Rudbeckia fulgida*
- *Salvia nemorosa*
- *Sanguisorba officinalis*
- *Scabiosa columbaria*
- *Verbascum* species (shown being planted here)

1 PREPARE FOR SOWING

Seed can be sown in late summer, leaving young plants to over-winter, or in early spring. Sow in clean seed trays or module trays with 62mm (2½in) cells. Use a loam-based seed compost, and create a level surface.

2 SOW THE SEED

Sow seed evenly. Lightly cover with compost as directed on the seed pack, and keep moist until seedlings appear. When large enough to handle prick out (see p.53) and grow on. In summer, when plants are large enough, plant out.

3 BUY IN PLUG-PLANTS

Instead of raising them from seed, many perennials can be bought ready established in small cell trays. Known as 'plug-plants', they can be planted out directly or grown on for planting in late summer.

4 PLANT OUT PLUGS

Set out plants, such as *Digitalis*, *Verbascum*, or *Primula*, in groups of three, five or seven, depending on space. Or add them to gaps in borders. Plant densely at first; thin as they knit together. Water after planting.

⑤ ENCOURAGING SELF-SEEDING

Once established, water only during droughts. Allow plants to self-seed to increase the effect year on year at no extra cost. Thin out the palette of plants according to taste and how well the various species are thriving. Remove the faded flower heads of plants that start to over-dominate, before they set seed.

RIGHT Exuberant displays of perennials and annuals makes an impressive summer show. Annuals are often added to perennial mixes to guarantee colour in the first year after sowing.

WILDLIFE BENEFITS

- Valuable food and habitat for pollinators, especially bees, butterflies and hoverflies
- Provides overwintering sites for insects and seeds for winter birds

GROWING TIPS

- Water seedlings during prolonged periods of drought until established.
- Remove any obvious weeds as they develop
- In future years, thin out any perennials that become over-dominant

DIRECT SOWING TECHNIQUE

Seed can also be sown directly onto the soil, but creating a low-fertility seedbed is preferable. First, remove the top 10–15cm (4–6in) layer of topsoil and set to one side. Then dig out a further 10–15cm (4–6in) and set aside. Fill the hole with the topsoil and then add the lower subsoil so that it is uppermost. Alternatively, spread a 5–10cm (2–4in) layer of subsoil over the soil surface and sow on that. For small areas, sow on a 2.5cm (1in) layer of horticultural sand or loam-based seed compost spread over the soil. To make sowing easier mix the seed with silver sand and scatter evenly over the surface.

laying meadow mats

READY-TO-USE WILDFLOWER MATS or turf rolls are very easy to use, and ideal for beginners or those wishing to establish a meadow quickly. The turves are created by sowing seed onto compost, which is held in place by a mesh base on a permeable plastic sheet. If you plan to use turf, you may need to pre-order it a few weeks or months in advance, particularly if it is being grown specifically for you.

Although, in theory, turves can be installed at any time of year, they are best laid in autumn, late winter or spring when the ground is moist. If laid in drier weather, water the ground beforehand and irrigate the turves until established. Before laying turf, prepare the ground well in advance (see pp.50–51). Rake over the area and fill any depressions to level the site and ensure the turf roots will be in contact with the soil. Turves can be heavy and if this will be a problem for you, ask the supplier about turf-laying services or to recommend a landscaping company that can carry out the work.

The supplier will advise on when, how and at what height the meadow turf should be mown. The timing usually allows some plants to re-seed, so that they will bloom again the following year. Remove and compost the clippings to prevent them smothering the weaker plants and fertilising the ground, and do not use any fertilisers unless the supplier recommends it.

Meadow turf will tolerate light foot traffic, but if you need to walk across it regularly, add permanent stepping stones or paving. Alternatively, mow a route regularly to create a short turf pathway through the flowery mix.

FACTORS TO CONSIDER BEFORE INSTALLING TURF ROLLS AND MEADOW MATS

Ideal for:
- Domestic lawns
- Slopes and larger areas where meadow turf will help stabilise changes of level
- Range of options for different sites
- Provides quick, yet long-term planting solutions
- Can be used in small or large areas

Advantages
- Landscape effects are instant and predictable
- Generally weather resistant
- Relatively easy to install and maintain

Disadvantages
- More expensive than other wildflower products
- Heavy to handle and position
- Can look untidy in winter if the main lawn feature

LAYING WILDFLOWER TURF ROLLS

These are as easy to lay as standard grass and provide an instant effect. Buy 'off-the-peg' or bespoke turf for specific needs.

SITE: Full sun or part shade
SOIL: Moist, free-draining
MAINTENANCE NEEDED: Low/medium

YOU WILL NEED
- Wildflower turf roll of choice
- Rake to level surface
- Wooden planks
- Half-moon cutter and rope or hosepipe
- Hose or watering can
- Rotary lawnmower

PLANT CHOICES

Turf roll options:
- Native wildflower turf
- Wildflowers for bees and butterflies
- Cottage garden turf
- Bespoke options for particular needs

1 STORING WILDFLOWER TURF

Pre-watered turf is delivered ready-rolled on pallets. These are substantially heavier than normal rolls of turf, so have extra help on hand to carry and lay it. Turf can remain stacked for a few days in a cool, shady area.

2 SITE PREPARATION

Prepare the site in advance (see pp. 50–51), removing perennial weeds and stones. Create a level, firm surface and soak the soil with a hose on a gentle spray beforehand if dry. Position the first line of turf across the site.

3 LAYING THE TURVES

Press each turf into the soil, ensuring the edge butts up firmly to the preceding one. Pack soil along the joints and beneath the edges if levels are slightly misaligned to ensure the turves root and knit together.

4 STAGGER THE ROWS

After laying the first line of turf, stand on a plank of wood to spread your weight and help prevent compaction. Stagger spacing of the next row so joints resemble a brick wall. Continue until the area is filled.

5 FINISHING TOUCHES

Firm in joints gently with your foot. Trim edges to shape as required using a half-moon turf-cutter. For sinuous curves, use a length of rope or hosepipe as a template. Water well and continue to water until the turf is well established.

ABOVE The wildflower turf should flower the first year after laying, if installed in spring, but may produce more floriferous effects in the second and subsequent years.

WILDLIFE BENEFITS
- Food for insect larvae and pollinating insects
- Food for birds and wildlife in autumn
- Habitat for insects, larvae, amphibians, reptiles and larger wildlife

GROWING TIPS
- Remove weeds before laying and as they appear
- Keep the turf watered in dry periods until fully established
- Mow twice a year as advised by the supplier and remove the trimmings

naturalising plants
in grassland

4

Seeds of ox-eye daisies have been sown into the grass each year, and then left to self-seed after flowering. To maintain this effect, allow the lawn to grow long and mow it in late summer, removing the clippings to reduce the soil fertility.

wild lawns and grasslands

❛ Longer grass is highly valuable for wildlife, with many kinds of insect and invertebrate using it as a refuge, food source or an environment in which to complete their life-cycles. ❜

Transforming a standard lawn into a miniature meadow is quick and easy. You can simply allow the grass to grow longer and see what other plants pop up in between, or plant robust perennials or bulbs for a more calculated effect.

Allow your lawn to go wild

A wide range of dramatic meadow-like effects can be created simply by letting your lawn grow a little longer. You do not have to treat the whole lawn in this way; select areas around trees or shrubs or allow just the edges to grow taller. If space allows, you could also be creative with your mower and use it to mark out swirls of shorter and longer grass or cut pathways through longer turf to create a meadow-like look. Even grass just a few inches taller than the standard length will produce a striking and attractive effect.

Longer grass is highly valuable for wildlife, with many kinds of insect and invertebrate using it as a refuge, food source or an environment in which to complete their various life-cycles. You can also augment turf and meadow areas with a host of exotic and native plants for a flowery meadow effect, which will boost the colour quota and add to the habitats in your wild garden.

Grassland encompasses such a wonderful, flexible community of plants and it is easily managed due to the unique way in which grasses grow and regenerate. Their growing point is at the base of the stem, rather than the tip, as is the case with most plants. This means that grasses can be cut without being damaged, and always strive to grow back to their natural height. Constant mowing prevents them from doing this and they

BELOW Native British bluebells (*Hyacinthoides non-scripta*) pepper a grassy meadow beneath an apple orchard in spring. Bluebells are easily established from young plants, after which they will self-seed and naturalise.

remain in an immature leafy state, which we can walk on. Grasses also expand by 'tillering', or producing side shoots, and the way in which they do this differs from species to species. Some are tight and compact, producing tufts of growth, while others are more vigorous, with a much looser, open habit, but they all knit together to produce a lush evergreen tapestry.

Various blends of grasses are used to create particular types of grassland. Shorter species and varieties make up lawn turf, while more vigorous, taller grasses are ideal for meadows.

Creating space for flowers

Rich green grassland is produced when there is an abundance of soil moisture and nutrients, such as nitrogen, which encourage soft, rampant growth. Conversely, grass growing on free-draining and naturally nutrient-poor soil is usually shorter and not as lush. Mowing and removing the clippings also checks the vigour of the grasses. This process lets in more light and opens up areas, exposing small patches of bare earth into which wildflowers can colonise and thrive. In lawns this usually takes the form of rosette plants, such as dandelions and daisies, or creeping species like speedwell, which can survive below the level of the cut. In meadows, dandelions also appear, along with buttercups, cranesbills, ox-eye daisies and a host of other species.

These naturally occurring flowers can be augmented with a variety of wildflowers, bulbs, perennials, and shrubs and trees, creating a long-lasting display of flowers, berries and seed heads almost all year round.

LEFT Rough turf left to grow long has taken on a character of its own in this garden. Wildflowers have started to colonise and the naturalised trees will eventually form a woodland glade.

RIGHT Lupins will naturalise in rough, open grassland where competition from the grass is low. Young plants will need protection from the ravages of slugs and snails until established.

BOTTOM LEFT Show restraint when selecting colours for your naturalised plants. A simple palette of just one colour, such as this drift of white daffodils, creates a more natural effect and heightens the drama.

BOTTOM RIGHT Single-flowered rambling roses can be used in short grass and will add a touch of floral exuberance when naturalised against a tree. Plant the rose away from the trunk and tie shoots to it with soft twine until they take hold by themselves.

Bulbs will produce a succession of blooms from winter through to late spring or early summer and, once planted, they need little or no aftercare to produce their annual displays.

ABOVE Robust species and varieties of crocus, such as *C. chrysanthus* and *C. tommasinianus,* will produce spangles of vibrant colour from late winter in short-mown grassland or a lawn. Gently drop handfuls of bulbs to the ground and plant where they fall for a more natural effect.

OPPOSITE LEFT Snake's-head fritillary *Fritillaria meleagris,* looks elegant when naturalised in damp grass. Established plants in pots, rather than dry bulbs, will establish more successfully.

OPPOSIT RIGHT *Tulipa sprengeri* is one of the few tulips that can be naturalised in open grassland, as shown here in the dappled shade beneath a tree. Mow the grass in late summer and autumn after the bulbs have flowered and the foliage has died down.

decorating turf with spring bulbs

LAWNS SPANGLED WITH BRIGHT spring bulbs are an early season delight and the effect is easily created in gardens of any size. Many bulbs or bulbous plants lend themselves to naturalising, which means that they propagate themselves via seed or offsets to produce self-sustaining communities. When grouped together, they will produce a succession of blooms from winter through to late spring or early summer, and, once planted, they need little or no aftercare to produce their annual displays.

Whichever bulbs you decide to plant, remember that the turf must remain unmown until the foliage of the final bulb in the sequence has started to wither or die down. Cutting before this process is complete will gradually deplete the energy reserves of the bulbs, causing them to fade away. Another cutting option if your bulbs are not planted too close together or they are set out in clumps, is to trim the grass around them with a strimmer, taking care not to decapitate or damage the bulbs as you do so, but you may find it more difficult to remove the grass clippings afterwards.

Plant in autumn

Spring-flowering bulbs are planted in autumn, as are those that flower in early summer, such as alliums and camassias. This allows them sufficient time to establish before they bloom.

Before planting, mow the area of turf or grassland to 5–7cm (2–3in) to make planting easier. Estimate the number of bulbs you need per square metre to create an impact and shop around for the best prices; most suppliers offer a discount for bulk buys or permit purchases at wholesale rates for large orders. That said, buy from a reputable source, and ensure the bulbs are good quality stock.

Avoid end-of-season 'job lots' of mixed bulbs, such as narcissi, as these are often of much lower quality and won't necessarily flower or perform as well, since they will also be planted late. When your bulbs arrive, check that they are firm and show no sign of fungal disease; discard any that are mouldy to prevent further infection.

Keep a check on growth

Although bulb displays in grass are among the easiest, cheapest and most rewarding schemes you can create, you have to plant them en masse to achieve a dramatic impact, so be prepared to be on your knees for some time and have the knee protectors at the ready! Once planted, keep a watch for signs of growth over winter. During mild winters, if the lawn or grass is still growing and the bulbs have not yet appeared, you can give it another cut, as long as the ground is not frozen or waterlogged. This will ensure that when your flowers do appear the following spring, the grass does not overwhelm them.

RECOMMENDED BULBS FOR NATURALISING

Choose naturalistic-looking bulbs and species or varieties that have the 'wild' look. Avoid tulips, which do not thrive in grass, apart from the smaller species recommended here.

- **Narcissus species:** *N. pseudonarcissus, N. lobularis* and *N. obvallaris* are dainty species. The small-headed 'Jack Snipe', 'Jetfire', and 'W. P. Milner' are also suitable for naturalising in turf.
- **Cyclamen species:** Autumn-flowering *C. hederifolium* and spring-flowering *C. coum* prefer the dry conditions beneath trees. Plant the crowns of the kidney-shaped tubers level with the soil surface.
- **Bluebells:** *Hyacinthoides non-scripta* will naturalise in dappled shade in woodland or moist, open grassland.

- **Tulip species:** *Tulipa saxatilis, T. sylvestris* and *T. sprengeri* can be successful in short, open turf, the latter even thriving in light, dappled shade beneath a tree.
- **Anemone species:** *Anemone blanda* flowers in spring and is suitable for moist shade. Low mats of dissected leaves are covered in daisy-like flowers in shades of blue, mauve and white. The white-flowered native *A. nemorosa* also flowers in spring and soon naturalises – try it beneath trees.
- **Snowdrops:** *Galanthus nivalis, G. elwesii* and *G.* 'S. Arnott' are good choices for grass. Rather than planting snowdrops as bulbs, plant them in leaf, known as 'in the green', in late spring after flowering. Buy from specialist suppliers via mail order or in pots.

PLANTING BULBS IN TURF

Spring and autumn bulbs in turf are among the most rewarding, as they flower when little else is in bloom. Once planted, they need very little aftercare.

SITE: Full sun or part shade
SOIL: Free-draining
MAINTENANCE NEEDED: Low

YOU WILL NEED

- Bulb species and varieties suitable for naturalising (see below)
- Narrow trowel or bulb planter
- Kneeler or knee protectors (optional, but a good investment if planting large areas)

PLANT CHOICES

Most species and cultivars of the following bulbs are suitable for growing in turf:
- *Allium*
- *Camassia*
- *Chionodoxa*
- *Colchicum*
- *Crocus*
- *Fritillaria*
- *Leucojum*
- *Muscari*
- *Narcissus* (above)
- *Scilla*

1 CHOOSE HEALTHY BULBS
Buy good quality, healthy bulbs, which are firm and show no signs of disease. Either plant a single type for a uniform effect or different species to provide a succession of blooms. Plant all spring bulbs at the same time so you can see where everything is.

2 SCATTER RANDOMLY
Mow turf before planting in autumn for spring and summer bulbs, or in summer for autumn bulbs. To give a more natural effect, gently drop handfuls of bulbs to the ground, and plant where they land (adjusting if too close).

3 REMOVE PLUG OF SOIL
Remove a core of turf and soil with a sharp narrow-bladed trowel. Bulbs should be planted at a depth of at least twice their height (see box right).

4 PLANT POINTED END UP
Place one bulb in each hole, ensuring that the pointed tip is facing upwards and the flatter area, from which the roots will grow, is at the bottom.

⑤ FINISHING TOUCHES

Replace the core of turf and press into position. Spring- and summer-flowering bulbs will make roots during the cool, moist days of autumn. Once planted, you do not need to water the bulbs in, as the winter or spring rain and soil moisture will be sufficient to enable the bulbs to establish.

BULB PLANTING DEPTHS

Most bulbs are planted two to three times as deep as the height of the bulb. For example, a narcissus bulb that measures 5cm (2in) from the base to the tip, will be planted at a depth of 10–15cm (4–6in), and a 2cm (¾in) *Muscari* bulb should be planted 4–6cm (1½–2¼in) deep.

ABOVE RIGHT A grassy meadow full of naturalised crocuses is a captivating sight and a feature that has long inspired gardeners around the world. The range and type of bulbs used in such plantings can be adapted to suit a wide range of habitat conditions.

WILDLIFE BENEFITS

- Food for early flying pollinating insects
- Food for some birds in spring and autumn

GROWING TIPS

- In normal conditions, there is no need to water in the bulbs once planted
- You can apply a spring lawn fertiliser after the bulbs have died down

❶ Snowdrops will tolerate short turf as well as more open situations.

❷ Small dainty daffodil species and varieties will give a natural air.

❸ Two colour variants of *Muscari* paint a dramatic picture in short turf.

❹ Large allium varieties will naturalise in open grassland.

❺ *Camassia* makes a vibrant show in taller grass in late spring.

❻ *Anemone blanda* will spread in open grassland in semi-shade.

❼ All scilla species are long-flowered companions for short grassland.

❽ *Crocus chrysanthus* and other vigorous hybrids suit lawn turf.

❾ *Erythronium dens-canis* thrives in open grassland beneath trees.

ABOVE TOP Buying plants as plugs minimises the cost of naturalising them in turf, if you don't have the space or time to sow seed. This mixed tray of primrose, mullein, foxglove and the herb, sainfoin, was bought online.

MIDDLE Plugs of great mullein, *Verbascum thapsus*, ready to plant in a border or open grassland.

BOTTOM Foxgloves are easy to naturalise and once established will soon flower and self-seed.

OPPOSITE Semi-double hollyhocks make a startling display in a gap between ornamental grasses.

naturalising biennials and perennials

ONE OF THE SEDUCTIVE ASPECTS of the traditional cottage garden is the drifts of self-sown biennials and short-lived perennials that pop up like familiar old friends. Allowing plants to self-seed can also be useful in the wild garden and in naturalistic plantings to help evoke an atmosphere of relaxed abandon. Bare patches of ground around shrubs, perennials or grassland can accommodate tough plants, such as aquilegia, foxgloves (*Digitalis*), mullein (*Verbascum*) and hollyhocks (*Alcea*), providing seasonal drama for free and with little effort.

Successful candidates

While it is easy to establish biennials and perennials in borders or gaps in naturalistic schemes where there is little or no competition, planting in grassland is more challenging, but worth exploring. Long-lived perennials are used more than biennials or shorter-lived perennials, although many species of *Verbascum* or hollyhock (*Alcea rugosa*) are able to thrive in shorter turf. The key to success hinges on your choice of perennials, which must be more vigorous and be able to out-compete constantly encroaching grasses. The best candidates, such as *Rheum* and *Symphytum*, possess long roots, which enable them to tap into deeper reserves of nutrients and water during dry periods, while plants at the surface, including grasses, struggle. Other species that survive in grassland have tough, fibrous rootstocks, which grasses find difficult to penetrate, or, like *Solidago*, they spread quickly to produce a stand of tall shoots.

Growth habit also contributes to the successful establishment of plants in grassland. Rosettes of leaves, such as those of *Verbascum*, create an open area by suppressing grasses in the immediate vicinity. Others, like *Veronicastrum* or *Solidago*, produce shoots that grow faster and taller than surrounding vegetation, while geraniums and everlasting peas (*Lathyrus latifolius*) produce trailing stems that clamber or weave through the jungle of grass shoots.

Keeping the grass in check

Some of these perennials may be too vigorous in the open garden, but in grassland they can compete adequately while their naturally expansive tendencies are kept in check. These plants are also able to access light, water and nutrients more effectively than the grasses, particularly in times of stress, such as during summer droughts. However, it is important to remove the immediate competition from the grasses when establishing perennials, either by stripping away a layer of turf to give the plants space to grow, or by careful use of weedkillers, such as glyphosate, beforehand to kill the grass.

NATURALISING BIENNIALS AND PERENNIALS

Bold perennials in open grassland make an impressive sight and offer an easy-care option if you choose tough plants that can compete.

SITE: Full sun or part shade
SOIL: Any except wet
MAINTENANCE NEEDED: Low/medium

YOU WILL NEED

- Suitable perennials (see below)
- Fork, spade, pickaxe or crowbar
- Bark chips for mulching
- Systemic weedkiller (optional)
- Strimmer or mower

PLANT CHOICES

- *Aster* (tall species)
- *Centaurea*
- *Cynara*
- *Eupatorium*
- *Geranium* (larger species)
- *Inula*
- *Lathyrus latifolius*
- *Malva moschata* (above)
- *Rheum*
- *Sanguisorba*
- *Solidago*
- *Symphytum*
- *Telekia*
- *Verbascum* (planted here)
- *Veronicastrum*

❶ CLEAR THE AREA

Mark out the area to be planted and strip off the surface layer of turf. You should also weed the area before planting to remove all perennial weeds, such as bindweed, couch grass, and dandelions, which will compete with the perennials (see p.51).

❷ RELIEVE COMPACTION

Dig over the area to relieve compaction. If the ground is hard or stony, use a pickaxe or crowbar to break it up, and remove the larger stones. Where the soil is impoverished, dig in well-rotted compost, but do not add any fertiliser.

❸ PLANT YOUR PERENNIALS

Plant in autumn and ensure the plants are healthy and large enough to establish quickly. Plant densely to create weed-proof clumps. Water plants in well and again during dry spells.

❹ CONTROL WEEDS

Surround plants with a bark-chip mulch to prevent weed growth and retain moisture. If perennial weeds appear in the planted area, apply weedkiller with a dab-on pad or paint-on brush.

⑤ MANAGE THE GRASSLAND

Until plants are fully established and growing well, keep down the vigour of the surrounding grassland. Cut it periodically with a strimmer or lawnmower, and remove the clippings. Do not apply any fertilisers, which will encourage grass growth at the expense of the plants.

PLANTING TIPS

When using bare-root plants in autumn, spread out the roots in the planting hole. If buying plants in pots, avoid any that are pot-bound, as they will be slow to root into the soil. Success will depend on maintaining the perennials' vigour over that of the grassland by removing weeds.

ABOVE RIGHT The tall, late summer-flowering plant, Joe Pye weed (*Eupatorium purpureum*), is a good choice for naturalising in rough, moist grassland.

WILDLIFE BENEFITS

- Food for a wide range of pollinating insects
- Seeds in autumn for birds
- Habitat and overwintering sites for insects

GROWING TIPS

- Leave plant stems over winter and cut down in spring before new growth commences
- Do not feed or water once plants have established; their roots will then expand to seek their own supplies

establishing trees and shrubs in grassland

NOTHING LOOKS QUITE AS ENCHANTING as a mature tree or large shrub with an underskirt of dewed grass, jewelled with wildflowers. While it may take a few years to achieve this vision, your patience will be rewarded with a beautiful, enduring feature.

In the natural world, most grasslands will be colonised first by shrubs and then by trees, and will eventually evolve into woodland. The exceptions are some grassland ecosystems, such as prairies, where the trees and shrubs are destroyed periodically by fire or removed by foraging animals or humans. The trees and shrubs that initially appear among the grasses are known as 'pioneer species', their seeds brought in by birds or on the wind. Hawthorn, elderberry, birch, and sloe are examples of these woody plants; all are well adapted to thrive in grassland habitats and ideal for your wild garden at home.

Clearing the way

Although pioneer species will thrive in grassland habitats, you can help them to establish successfully and ensure they win the battle for supremacy over the grasses by leaving a clear area around them for the first year or two. A few weeks or months before planting, prepare the site by removing the grass in the planting area, either with a weedkiller or by digging out the turf by hand. When stripping off turf by hand, ensure you remove all the roots. Apply weedkiller (glyphosate) when the grass is actively growing from spring onwards – more than one application may be needed to kill the grass completely.

Planting trees and shrubs is best undertaken in autumn when the roots have time to develop in relatively warm soil so they will grow away strongly in spring. You can choose to plant larger, more expensive specimen trees, which will give an instant effect, or smaller, younger specimens that will often grow away faster. A grove of smaller trees will also knit together quickly to help shade out the grasses below. They can then be thinned once established.

Aftercare is as important as the planting methods used, and the grassland around your trees and shrubs may need to be kept in check for a year or two until it is shaded out. A bark-chip mulch will help to achieve this while also helping to keep the woody plants' roots moist.

OPPOSITE TOP The turf around this five-year-old fruit tree was stripped away when it was planted and is now controlled by mulching and weeding.

OPPOSITE BOTTOM Given proper care, many trees and shrubs can be established in grassland. They will eventually shade out or subdue the grasses, creating the space and light they need to fully develop and reach maturity.

NATURALISING TREES IN GRASS

Trees in grassland impart a timeless, romantic look to any garden and are easy to grow if you select species that suit your site.

SITE: Full sun, part or deep shade
SOIL: Any, except wet
MAINTENANCE NEEDED: Low

YOU WILL NEED

- Bare-root or container-grown trees of choice
- Spade, fork and shovel
- Slow-release general fertiliser
- Mycorrhizal root product
- Irrigation equipment
- Tree stakes and ties
- Mulching materials

PLANT CHOICES

- *Acer* (maple)
- *Betula* (birch)
- *Crataegus* (hawthorn)
- *Ilex* (holly)
- *Malus* (apple/crab apple)
- *Pyrus* (pear)
- *Sorbus*

WILDLIFE BENEFITS

- Food, shelter and habitat supporting the life-cycles of a wide variety of insects and invertebrates
- Feeding, nesting and roosting sites for birds

GROWING TIPS

- Water trees in prolonged drought, until established
- Check tree ties are secure and remove when tree is wind-firm
- Control weeds below the canopy and keep grass mown in this area too

1 PREPARE FOR PLANTING

Plant trees in autumn as grass becomes dormant and the tree has a better chance of establishing. Use bare-root or container-grown plants. A few weeks prior to planting, clear an area of grass at least 1m (39in) in diameter; use a weedkiller or strip off the turf by hand. You can also incorporate organic matter into the whole area prior to planting.

2 DIG A PLANTING PIT

Make a hole at least 30cm (12in) wider but no deeper than the tree's root ball or spread of roots. Loosen soil at the sides of the hole with a fork. Position the tree in the centre of the planting hole.

3 PLANT THE TREE

Ensure the tree's root ball is positioned at the same level in the soil as it was in its pot or, for bare-root specimens, when growing in its nursery bed. You can also apply a mycorrhizal root product to encourage root development. Young trees do not generally need staking but if planting a mature specimen, add a stake next to the root ball on the windward side. Fill the hole and firm in the soil around the roots. Water thoroughly and apply a thick mulch of bark chips over the planted area. Apply a tree guard against rodents or deer if required. (See pp.56–57 for further tree-planting advice)

1 Rowan or sorbus trees are good food sources for wildlife and ideal for grassland.

2 False indigo, *Amorpha fruticosa*, is a common plant of the American prairies.

3 Species of *Solidago* add spots of colour.

4 Robust species of *Inula* make a bold feature in grass in high summer.

5 Clumps of *Crocosmia* offer a colourful spectacle in short grassland.

6 Sumach, *Rhus typhina*, forms suckering colonies in long turf.

7 Mature apple trees make an attractive feature in a grassy meadow.

8 Aquilegia soon self-seeds in meadows.

9 Hawthorn, (*Crataegus*), is a good choice for colonising long grass.

naturalistic plantings

5

The vibrant partnering of purple *Agastache*, pink *Origanum* 'Rosenkuppel', pink *Prunella grandiflora*, *Sedum* and *Penstemon digitalis* 'Husker Red' creates a summer spectacle punctuated by ornamental grasses.

‘ Everything from copses of sculptural trees through to drifts of miniature bulbs can be artfully placed and combined to create an enhanced sense of nature. ’

enhancing nature

Take inspiration from natural plant communities to create relaxed drifts of colour, form and texture in borders or the wider garden. The plants will provide food and habitat for wildlife while creating year-round interest for you to enjoy.

Achieving your creative vision

Using blends of native and exotic plants, you can mimic the way in which plant communities and natural features appear in the wild. Everything from copses of sculptural trees through to drifts of miniature bulbs can be artfully placed to create an enhanced sense of nature, while at the same time encouraging more wildlife to use what's on offer. Each particular community or feature requires you to carefully analyse your conditions (see pp.46–48) to ensure that the approach you are intending is sustainable in terms of climate and soil, and your chosen plants will establish and thrive.

Although it is best to work with your environmental conditions and use an approach appropriate to your site, you can make adaptations to suit your vision. For example, you may wish to plant more trees and shrubs to provide shelter, thin out branches to let in more light or enlarge a small depression to create a pond. But you will be limited by the space available and must manage your expectations. If developing a small garden, for instance, creating a wild prairie grassland will be a challenge, as it will be difficult to achieve the desired grand sweep of planting. However, by carefully selecting plants that are compact or upright in habit, and perhaps including a path meandering through the plants, you will be able to sketch out something that captures the atmosphere of a mighty floral grassland. By carefully planning schemes in advance, it will be possible to fulfil most of your ambitions.

TOP RIGHT Forms of *Miscanthus sinensis* have attractive flowers and seed heads that last into winter, prolonging the season of interest. Ideal for prairie-like effects, team them with tall daisy- or airy-flowered perennials.

RIGHT A Japanese-style boardwalk picks its way through a glade of young birch trees, below which are informal groupings of *Dryopteris* ferns, ornamental grasses and shade-tolerant evergreen and deciduous shrubs.

creating prairie-style schemes

RELAXED GROUPS OF COLOURFUL yet wild-looking perennials and ornamental grasses that generate the look and feel of meadows have become all the rage in recent years. These designs take inspiration from the major grassland habitats of the world, such as the American prairies and central European steppes, which include a huge diversity of flowering perennials and grasses. In the garden, the idea is to mimic these self-sustaining communities of plants to provide colour and structure from spring onwards, with a peak of interest in summer and autumn, and continuing on into winter with ornamental seed heads and sere stems. Old growth is then cut down and removed in spring as fresh stems and leaves appear.

Tough plant selections

The perennials in prairie-style schemes are chosen for their durability and persistence in a wide range of conditions. Disease resistance, visual presence, especially in winter, a long flowering period and an unaggressive, clump-forming habit are the qualities you should look for. The grass species used have similar physical characteristics to the perennials, but are also chosen for their beautiful flower heads and foliage, as well as their structure, especially in autumn and winter. Most of the plants are long-lasting, but they may require lifting, splitting and replanting every three or four years.

The structure of the planting can be varied according to taste, but tends to comprise carpets or rivers of smaller perennials through which taller, more upright varieties emerge to create different shapes and forms. The filigree flower heads of grasses, such as *Stipa gigantea* and *Deschampsia cespitosa* 'Bronzeschleier', provide a see-through gossamer veil. The effects can be carefully manicured using a restricted palette of species, perhaps with a colour theme, or with more riotous abandon, using clashing colours and billowing forms. Spring and early summer bulbs help to fill in gaps early in the year and provide colour while the majority of the plants get into gear. Alliums are particularly useful, as they not only provide dramatic spheres of pink, mauve, purple or white flowers, but also attractive seed heads.

Sculptural grasses

Many of the grasses, such as *Miscanthus*, *Molinia* and *Panicum*, announce their presence from late summer with airy or plume-like flowers. As autumn progresses the stems become dry and sere, or like *Panicum virgatum* 'Shenandoah' or *Miscanthus* 'Red Chief', turn scarlet before fading. The seed heads and dried stems of the whole confection make a dramatic statement through winter, particularly when dusted with frost. In late winter, simply cut down the stems or comb through the foliage of evergreen grasses and start the cycle again.

PLANT A PRAIRIE-STYLE BORDER

Inspired by the billowing flower-studded grasslands of the North-American prairies, these designs can be created in gardens large and small.

SITE: Full sun
SOIL: Free-draining, normal
MAINTENANCE NEEDED: Low

YOU WILL NEED

- Selection of perennials and ornamental grasses
- Border fork and trowel
- Irrigation equipment
- Mulching materials

PLANT CHOICES

Perennials
- *Allium* species
- *Aster* species
- *Echinacea* species
- *Helenium* species
- *Monarda* species
- *Rudbeckia* species
- *Salvia nemorosa* (above)
- *Sedum spectabile*

Grasses
- *Deschampsia cespitosa*
- *Miscanthus sinensis*
- *Molinia caerulea*
- *Panicum* species
- *Schizachyrium scoparium*
- *Stipa* species

1 PREPARE THE GROUND

Clear the ground of perennial weeds beforehand. Prepare the ground, digging over the surface if compacted. Also remove any annual weed growth just prior to planting (see p.51) so the ground is clear.

2 SET OUT PLANTS IN DRIFTS

Choose plants that are suited to your soil conditions and climate. Estimate the number needed to fill the allotted space after two year's growth. Set them out in intersecting groups (see left) of grasses and perennials, mixing early- and later-flowering types.

3 PLANT INDIVIDUALLY

Dig a hole for each plant and fork over the bottom of the pit. Tease out the plant roots and place in the hole with the neck of the plant positioned at ground level. Back-fill the hole with soil and firm in. There is no need to add fertiliser.

4 ADD BULBS IN BETWEEN

In autumn, plant bulbs in small clumps or singly at a depth two to three times their height (see pp.86–87). Label their positions. After everything is planted soak the area. Water again in dry spells until plants are well established.

ABOVE In a damp but well-drained soil, pink cone flowers, including the droopy-petalled *Echinacea pallida*, blend with spotted bee balm, *Monarda punctata* and *Verbena bonariensis* above a golden mist of ponytail grass, *Stipa tenuissima*.

WILDLIFE BENEFITS

- Food for pollinating insects in spring and summer
- Food for birds and wildlife in autumn
- Habitat and food for insect and invertebrate larvae

GROWING TIPS

- Remove weeds regularly
- Thin or divide overgrown plants every few years
- Remove faded flowers unless leaving them to self-seed
- Cut down and remove old stems,and comb through evergreens, in early spring

PRAIRIE-STYLE PLANTING PLANS

MELDING ORNAMENTAL GRASSES with perennials in informal groups can create drama and potent visual interest, ranging from subtle to bold effects. The trick is to use clump-forming, upright plants that have more than one season of interest, such as structural shape and form all year, flowers in summer and autumn seed heads.

Roof-top medley

The interplay between the purple foliage of *Sedum* with silvery, shrubby *Convolvulus* creates interest from spring to late autumn and beyond, while pastel floral highlights from many of the plants reach a crescendo in late summer.

Grow these plants in full sun and free-draining soil. The dried stems and seed heads of the perennials can be left over winter and cut down in early spring when the new growth emerges.

ROOF-TOP MEDLEY: PLANTS USED

❶ *Lavandula angustifolia* 'Hidcote'

❷ *Sedum* 'Matrona'

❸ *Achillea* 'Kelwayi'

❹ *Stipa tenuissima*

❺ *Convolvulus cneorum*

❻ *Erigeron karvinskianus*

High-summer fiesta

North-American grassland perennials set among
clump-forming ornamental grasses, such as
Calamagrostis x *acutiflora* and *Panicum virgatum*,
reach their flowering peak from mid- to late
summer. The pert yellow daisies of the black-eyed
Susan *Rudbeckia fulgida* var *speciosa* and taller,
lax-petalled prairie coneflower, *Ratibida pinnata*,
form the mainstay, while contrasting floral highlights
are provided by the purple prairie gayfeather,
Liatris spicata, and scarlet royal catchfly, *Silene
regia*. Long-flowered, the rudbeckias prolong the
display into late summer, especially if they are
deadheaded, after which the seed heads and
autumnal tones of the ornamental grasses provide
visual interest into winter.

Cut down the dried stems of both perennials
and grasses in spring and in autumn plant spring
and early summer bulbs, such as scillas and alliums,
to fill the void earlier in the year. All the plants thrive
in full sun, and moist but free-draining soil.

HIGH-SUMMER FIESTA: PLANTS USED

❶ *Liatris spicata*
❷ *Ratibida pinnata*
❸ *Calamagrostis* x *acutiflora* 'Karl Foerster'
❹ *Silene regia*
❺ *Rudbeckia fulgida* var *speciosa*

Mediterranean inspirations

LANDSCAPES DOMINATED BY SILVER, dark green, or soft-leaved evergreen shrubs, drifts of aromatic perennials, dazzling spring bulbs and tough grasses encapsulate the look of the Mediterranean maquis. This drought-tolerant plant community provides the template for a range of naturalistic plantings, even in wetter, more temperate climes. As well as plants from the Mediterranean, you can augment your designs with the distinctive flora found in similar climatic zones, such as the Californian chaparral and South African fynbos.

The Mediterranean climate is generally dry, hot and sunny in summer, with just a little rainfall in winter and early spring, while the soils are very well drained and often nutrient-poor, or very alkaline or acidic. Temperatures vary but rarely fall below -3°C (27°F). Many plants from this region grow successfully in cooler areas, but the soil must remain well-drained in winter for them to survive. One of the best examples of a cool-climate Mediterranean planting is the gravel garden at the renowned Beth Chatto Gardens in Essex, an area of the UK that experiences cold winters but low annual rainfall.

Sun seekers

To create the look, try silver-leaved shrubs, such as *Artemisia* and *Santolina*, with fleshy sedums and crassulas, compact euphorbias, salvias, and blue fescues, and stately yuccas, set out in swirling borders coated with a gravel mulch. These plants are beautiful for most of the year, and you can add to them with herbs, such as lavender and rosemary, and a blue-flowered *Ceanothus* trained against a wall.

Plants from Mediterranean climates share a suite of characteristics, such as grey, felted leaves, which may be narrow, spear-shaped or aromatic. Succulents, including the sedums and crassulas, have thick, fleshy foliage, often covered in wax or dusted with farina, which protects them from sun scorch. These sun-lovers also have ground-hugging, mounded or gaunt habits, and tend to be compact.

Spring charms

Bulbs, corms or rhizomes from the Mediterranean appear in spring after the rains, but escape summer drought by retreating underground. These plants need excellent drainage and will not tolerate excessive moisture around their roots in winter, which will cause them to rot. Free-draining soils, such as sand or chalk, create more hospitable conditions for bulbs than clay, even if it dries in summer. You can work grit or gravel into clay soil to increase the drainage or plant in raised beds. Some bulbs, such as *Crinum*, *Eucomis* and gladiolus are not fully hardy in cold areas, and unless grown in a sheltered spot, they will need winter protection with a mulch of bark or straw. Or lift and store them in a cool place indoors, and plant out again in late spring.

PLANTING IN A MEDITERRANEAN STYLE

Redolent of summer holidays in the sun, Mediterranean-style plantings are ideal for sunny, sheltered spots and poor soils.

SITE: Full sun
SOIL: Free-draining
MAINTENANCE NEEDED: Low

YOU WILL NEED

- Selection of drought-tolerant, sun-loving trees, shrubs, herbs and bulbs
- Horticultural grit for clay or poorly drained soils
- Gravel for mulching (optional)
- Border fork and trowel
- Watering equipment

PLANT CHOICES

- *Allium*
- *Agapanthus*
- *Artemisia*
- *Asphodeline lutea*
- *Cistus*
- *Crocosmia*
- *Eryngium*
- *Euphorbia characias*
- *Iris germanica*
- *Lavandula*
- *Ozothamnus*
- *Phlomis*
- *Rosmarinus*
- *Salvia* (above)
- *Stachys byzantina*

① CREATE IDEAL CONDITIONS

Poor, well-drained sandy soil is ideal for plants from Mediterranean climates. Cold, wet conditions in winter will encourage frost damage and rots. Soil containing brick rubble or broken concrete from building works can be used without any additives. Improve the drainage of clay soil by digging in horticultural grit or plant in raised beds.

② USE YOUNG PLANTS

It is better to plant young shrubs and perennials, rather than use mature specimens, especially if you have stony ground. Young plants will adapt better to your conditions and their fine, questing roots will quickly search out water and nutrients. Do not apply any fertilisers when planting, but after planting, do water in thoroughly.

③ PRUNE SHRUBS ANNUALLY

Most Mediterranean plants are relatively maintenance-free, but most of the shrubs will benefit from light pruning after flowering to rejuvenate them and encourage new shoots to form. Shrubs with old or straggly growth often die prematurely, while some, such as *Cistus*, only live for a few years and will need replacing.

ABOVE A subtle blend of evergreen shrubs and herbaceous perennials, including *Eryngium*, *Stachys byzantina*, *Phlomis*, rosemary, hyssop and thyme, bring floral and aromatic accents to this sun-drenched courtyard.

WILDLIFE BENEFITS

- Valuable food for all pollinators, especially bees and butterflies
- Habitat and overwintering sites for insects
- Cover for small mammals

GROWING TIPS

- Rejuvenate flowering shrubs by clipping lightly after blooming. Do not hard prune as many will not regenerate from old stems
- Do not apply fertiliser as this will encourage soft growth

PLANTING PLANS FOR SUNNY RETREATS

TURN POOR, DRY SOIL in sun into a virtue by using plants that luxuriate in these conditions. Colourful, with long-lasting visual interest, they also support a wide range of pollinators.

High and dry

This narrow, shallow planting bed in a roof-top garden uses a range of drought-tolerant perennials to provide form, texture and colour in a light, airy floral confection. Startling blue grass *Helictotrichon* and silvery lavender contrast with pink *Achillea* and purple-leaved *Heuchera*, while a cloud of pink-purple *Verbena bonariensis* flowers floats above. Other drought-tolerant grasses provide additional foliar pizzazz, injecting airy flowers from late summer. Plant these sun-lovers in spring in free-draining soil and full sun.

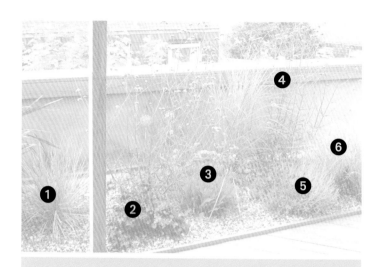

HIGH AND DRY: PLANTS USED

❶ *Helictotrichon sempervirens*

❷ *Heuchera* 'Chocolate Ruffles'

❸ *Achillea* 'Summerwine'

❹ *Verbena bonariensis*

❺ *Lavandula angustifolia* 'Hidcote'

❻ *Anemanthele lessoniana*

Rhapsody in blue

A bold, colour-themed planting of drought-tolerant perennials, such as the vivid blue *Salvia nemorosa* 'Caradonna' and scarlet *Lychnis,* together with globe-topped alliums, form a melee of blue, purple and vibrant red tones for many weeks in early summer. The salvias and scabious (*Scabiosa columbaria*) form the heart of the planting, and are contrasted with striking silver and white *Lychnis coronaria* 'Alba', which periodically bursts through the planting. This useful but short-lived plant will also self-seed into gaps. *Allium* 'Globemaster' enlivens the scene with an early summer blast of pinky-purple pompoms, which transmute into straw-coloured spiky seed heads that provide additional interest for the rest of the summer and sometimes into autumn.

Plant the perennials in spring or autumn in close-knit groups, and weave in the alliums, which should be planted in autumn, between them.

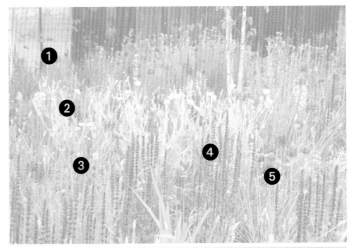

RHAPSODY IN BLUE: PLANTS USED

❶ *Allium* 'Globemaster'

❷ *Lychnis coronaria* 'Alba'

❸ *Knautia macedonica*

❹ *Salvia nemorosa* 'Caradonna'

❺ *Scabiosa columbaria*

creating miniature woodland glades

FEW GARDEN OWNERS have a woodland in which to make a glade, but you can create a woodland edge in an average-sized plot using small trees or shrubs. Beneath the tree canopy in a natural deciduous woodland is a layer of shade-tolerant shrubs and, below that, a covering of herbaceous plants, ferns, and bulbs, which mostly perform in late winter or early spring before the tree leaves unfurl. On the edge of a woodland, where there is additional light, moisture and nutrients, a wider range of plants thrive, forming an important wildlife habitat and natural ecosystem. Many gardens already have the makings of this plant community, with existing trees and shrubs or a shady area that shouts out for such a treatment.

Plant fusion

The layered effects seen in wild woodlands can be recreated in the garden in various ways, using native or exotic species, or a mixture of both. When choosing new trees to plant, select those that cast light shade, such as birch (*Beluta*), rowan (*Sorbus*) or snake-bark maples (*Acer davidii*). If you have existing trees that cast dense shade, consider lifting the canopy by removing lower branches or thinning out limbs. If you have no room or don't want to include trees, plant instead a range of evergreen and deciduous shrubs of different heights – you can train tall, vigorous shrubs to form tree-like forms by removing the lower branches. In narrow spaces, consider an informal row or 'hedge' of mixed native shrubs, such as the guelder rose (*Viburnum opulus*), hazel (*Corylus avellana*), spindle (*Euonymus europaeus*) and blackthorn (*Prunus spinosa*). Also try non-natives, including *Berberis* x *stenophylla*, *Lonicera* x *purpusii* or *Cotoneaster simonsii*. You can also turn this into a fruiting hedge that yields berries in summer and autumn for birds to feast on. Good choices for such a feature include cherry plums (*Prunus cerasifera*), fruiting forms of *Cornus mas*, saskatoons (*Amelanchier alnifolia*) and the clove currant (*Ribes odoratum*).

Perennials that love shade, especially moist shade, abound, and include *Brunnera*, *Epimedium*, *Heuchera*, and *Helleborus*, among others. Most flower from late winter to early summer, while biennial foxgloves will also seed around, providing a succession of stately spires. When planting for wildlife, use plants with single, rather than double, flowers. Ferns, such as *Athyrium*, *Dryopteris* and *Polystichum*, provide foils of lacy green foliage against which other woodland plants can shine, while spring bulbs, such as snowdrops, dwarf narcissi and scillas, can be planted around them and in gaps between plantings, where they will clump up and self-seed. Use bark chips throughout as a mulch to help keep down weeds and to retain soil moisture.

PLANTING A SLICE OF WOODLAND

Whether set around trees or in shaded areas, woodland plants will transform unlikely spaces into lush oases.

SITE: Part or deep shade
SOIL Normal to moist
MAINTENANCE NEEDED: Low

YOU WILL NEED

- Shade-tolerant plants
- Fork, spade and trowel
- Well-rotted organic matter
- Irrigation equipment

PLANT CHOICES

Dry shade
- *Alchemilla mollis*
- *Aster divaricatus*
- *Bergenia* species & varieties
- *Dryopteris* species
- *Geranium macrorrhizum*
- *Heuchera* varieties
- *Liriope* species
- *Luzula* species

Moist shade
- *Astrantia* species (above)
- *Astilbe* species & varieties
- *Brunnera macrophylla*
- *Epimedium* species
- Ferns - all types
- *Geum* varieties
- *Helleborus* species
- *Hydrangea* species

❶ ASSESS YOUR SITE

Evaluate the amount of light and rainfall reaching the ground as this influences the plants you can grow, broadly split into those tolerating dry or moist shade (see below left). Select a range of plants that sustain interest from late winter into summer, and a few evergreens, such as *Polystichum* ferns, for continuous colour.

❷ PREPARATION AND PLANTING

Dig plenty of well-rotted organic matter into the soil before planting, both to enrich it and improve its water-holding ability. Plant either pot-grown or bare-root trees, shrubs and perennials in either autumn or late winter. Plant winter and spring bulbs, such as snowdrops, *Eranthis*, *Erythronium* and narcissus, in autumn.

❸ POSITIONING AND AFTERCARE

Position plants so they receive sufficient light, and are not overwhelmed by taller neighbours. Use ground-cover plants, such as geraniums and epimedium, around taller shrubs, such as camellias, to help suppress weeds. Water in after planting, and in dry spells until plants are fully established (see also pp.56–57 for tree planting tips).

ABOVE In a small clearing among woodland shrubs, white-flowered *Lunaria rediviva*, dark-leaved *Lysimachia ciliata* 'Firecracker' and a skirt of *Geranium macrorrhizum* 'Spessart' make a lush display.

WILDLIFE BENEFITS

- Food for pollinating insects in spring and summer
- Habitat and food for insect and invertebrate larvae
- Habitat for amphibians and other shade-loving wildlife

GROWING TIPS

- Clear away dead stems in late summer or spring
- Mulch around plants every spring to keep down weeds and retain moisture
- Thin out or replace old or overly vigorous plants

WOODLAND PLANTING PLANS

TRANSFORM GLOOMY AREAS with shade-tolerant and woodland plants grouped together to emulate plant communities found in nature. Choose those that provide long-lasting interest through leaf form and texture, as well as flower.

Springtime symphony

This intimate slate seating area in a small garden is shrouded by shrubs and trees, such as viburnum, birch and field maple, and underplanted with an array of spring-flowering woodland plants. Golden daffodils, the spidery-flowered *Epimedium* and pink bergenias offer a floral spectacle, while the fresh foliage of variegated hostas and ferns offers additional impact and makes excellent leafy ground cover.

The whole display, including the bulbs, should be planted in the autumn.

SPRINGTIME SYMPHONY: PLANTS USED

❶ *Narcissus* - small forms
❷ *Bergenia* 'Overture'
❸ *Polystichum setiferum*
❹ *Hosta undulata* var *albomarginata*
❺ *Epimedium x versicolor* 'Sulphureum'

Cool combinations

Beneath the field maple, *Acer campestre*, and fringed by flower-spangled grassland, a range of perennial and biennial plants have been established to further boost this semi-wild effect. The bold jagged foliage of white-flowered *Ranunculus aconitifolius* and simple white foxgloves form an elegant partnership, while yellow Welsh poppy, *Meconopsis cambrica*, *Lunaria annua* 'Corfu Blue' and red campion, *Silene dioica*, provide a spattering of brighter tones. All will self-seed to create a succession of new plants in future years.

If any plants, such as the poppy, start to dominate the display, thin out individuals and remove the faded flower heads before they have a chance to set seed. All of these plants can be established in autumn or early spring, and they are also hardy, taking care of themselves with little further intervention after planting.

COOL COMBINATIONS: PLANTS USED

❶ *Silene dioica*

❷ *Lunaria annua* 'Corfu Blue'

❸ *Meconopsis cambrica*

❹ *Ranunculus aconitifolius*

❺ *Digitalis purpurea* f *albiflora*

making a naturalistic pond and bog garden

WATER IS A TRANSFORMATIVE ELEMENT for any wild garden, providing a beautiful and highly valuable habitat for wildlife. Before creating a pond or water feature, consider its size, where it should be sited, the method of construction and how water levels are to be maintained. The latter is an important factor; for it to be of real value to wildlife, ideally replenish it with rainwater rather than mains supplies. Topping up levels with fresh rainwater will also keep the pool in a better state of health and the water oxygenated. The smaller the pool, the more critical this will be, since the water will evaporate faster than in a larger feature. Edge treatments are also important. Gently sloping sides which are planted or turfed sit far more comfortably in a wild garden than geometric designs. A flexible butyl liner will also allow you greater creative freedom than a pre-formed fibreglass unit, enabling you to make a shape and form to suit the space.

Naturally wet areas of the garden could form the nucleus of a bog garden, or you could create one by burying a sheet of butyl liner a foot or so below the soil surface (see p.119 for instructions).

Rainy day pools

Another option is to make a rain garden, which is like a shallow pool where the water is stored temporarily after a storm, after which it is left to evaporate, seep away naturally, or run into a soakaway, so that the area remains dry between rainfall events. Connect the pool to the downpipe of a shed, summerhouse or the main house. Rain gardens are just as valuable to wildlife as pools, since many amphibians only need water at certain times of year to spawn. A shallow beach area will allow access to and from the water for birds and other wildlife.

6 Naturally wet areas of the garden could form the nucleus of a bog garden, or you could create one by burying a sheet of butyl liner a foot or so below the soil surface. 9

OPPOSITE A lushly planted pond has become a serene centrepiece for this garden, as well as creating an important habitat for many kinds of wildlife. The shelving around the margins of the pond and gently sloping sides enable plants to establish and develop a smooth transition to the rest of the garden.

BELOW The planting around a pond is as important as the planting in it, adding to the wildlife value of the whole feature. A mix of native and exotic plants will help to sustain pollinators, and provide sites for insects to lay eggs and the larvae to feed.

MAKING A WILD POND

You will need to set aside a few days to create a wildlife pond, but the end result will last a lifetime and dramatically increase the range of wildlife in your garden.

SITE: Full sun or part shade
MAINTENANCE NEEDED: Medium

YOU WILL NEED

- Butyl pond liner
- Spades, shovels
- Wheelbarrow to remove soil
- Soft sand or a specialist underlay to protect the liner
- Rocks and cobbles for decorative margins
- Washed gravel for beach areas
- Selection of pond plants
- Plastic close-mesh baskets for pond plants
- Loam-based aquatic compost

PLANT CHOICES

- *Butomus umbellatus*
- *Caltha palustris* (above)
- *Iris sibirica, Iris laevigata*
- *Orontium aquaticum*
- *Ranunculus lingua* 'Grandiflorus'
- *Saururus cernuus*
- *Typha minima*
- *Veronica beccabunga*
- Water lily for small/medium ponds

❶ DIG OUT A HOLE

Locate the pond in a sunny or semi-shaded position. Mark out the area with a length of rope or hose. Include a shallow beach zone around the edges with cobbles and gravel to enable wildlife to enter, and to create a more natural style. If you intend to keep fish, ensure the deepest part of the pool is at least 45cm (18in) for winter protection; a specialist supplier can advise about specific fish.

❷ CHECK THE LEVELS

Dig out the side of the pond and create shelves at various depths to suit the marginal plants you have chosen. Check levels across the edges of the site, as this will affect where the final water level will sit. This is important if you are to plant the margins or allow water to permeate into a boggy area. Remove any sharp stones that could puncture the liner, and compact the final shape with a spade or by hand.

❸ LAY THE LINER

Calculate the size of liner required beforehand, usually twice the area of the pond, but also include beach areas. Take advice if unsure. Pack soft sand over the pond surfaces to protect the liner or use a pond underlay. Position the liner and mould it around the contours, working from the centre out.

❹ FILL WITH WATER

Work in stockinged feet when standing on the liner. Once in position, add water, using rainwater if possible; otherwise use mains. Fill to the required level and allow the water to settle overnight. Check for any leaks before trimming off the margins to shape, leaving about 45cm (18in) around the sides.

POND PLANTING TIPS

Plants are a real asset to any pond, but they need planting with care. Use close-weave plastic mesh baskets, choosing sizes that allow plants room to grow to maturity. Always use a loam-based aquatic compost, rather than garden soil or potting compost, which contains too much soluble fertiliser or nutrients. Knock the plant out of its pot and carefully tease out some of the looser roots. Place it in the basket on a layer of compost; ensure the top of the root ball is about 2.5cm (1in) lower than the rim. Add more compost, firming it carefully around the roots to just below the neck of the plant. Add a 2.5cm (1in) layer of gravel on top. Gently lower the basket into the water to the plant's recommended depth, and adjust the position with terracotta path tiles.

⑤ EDGE TREATMENTS

Place baskets of plants on the shelves, adjusting their heights with tiles as required. Lay turf and washed cobbles and gravel around the sides. If using rocks position these before filling with water, and bed them on insulating felt to prevent punctures. You can make a bog garden with spare liner (see p.119).

WILDLIFE BENEFITS

- Important habitat for amphibians, invertebrates and insects
- Flowering plants offer food for pollinating insects
- Water source for birds and small mammals

POND CARE TIPS

- Top up level with rainwater when needed
- Remove autumn leaves and dead foliage annually
- Lift and divide overgrown pond plants in spring
- Every few years, clean out the pond and remove silt

ABOVE Evoking a stream-side setting with artfully placed rocks and stony beaches, this feature offers easy access for wildlife, such as amphibians, small mammals and birds.

BOG AND POND EDGE PLANTING PLANS

WHETHER YOUR POOL IS SMALL or large, planting around it will help anchor the feature into the landscape and bring it to life. Plants also boost the range of habitats for the many wild creatures that will be drawn to the water.

Bold and beautiful

Even modest pools benefit from bold plantings, such as this giant-leaved *Gunnera manicata*, providing an opulent, subtropical accent. A fringe of summer-flowering *Iris laevigata* contrasts with variegated hostas, and the decorative floating leaves of the water hawthorn, *Aponogeton distachyos*, create a seamless transition from the banks to the water.

Plant in spring. Cut down the *Gunnera* leaves and use them to cover the plant's roots in winter.

BOLD AND BEAUTIFUL: PLANTS USED

1 *Aponogeton distachyos*

2 *Iris laevigata*

3 *Gunnera manicata*

4 *Miscanthus sinensis*

5 *Hosta sieboldiana* 'Frances Williams'

Floral fireworks

In this pond-side setting, the unusual yellow Asian daisy *Arnica sachalinensis* provides a vibrant contrast against pink and red primulas, which are set next to the fine-leaved sedge (*Carex brizoides*).

Creating an area of wet or damp soil adjacent to a pond greatly expands the range of plants you can grow. You can do this artificially by laying a sheet of pond liner about 20–30cm (8–12in) below the soil surface around the edges of the pond. Make a few holes in the liner so that some water can drain out but most will be retained to keep the area damp. The water from the pool will periodically spill over the banks and into the soil in this area to create the boggy conditions required. You can also lay some capillary matting just below the soil surface, with one end dipped into the pond water. This will draw up moisture, also helping to keep the soil damp in the bog.

FLORAL FIREWORKS: PLANTS USED

1. *Mimulus guttatus*
2. *Primula beesiana*
3. *Carex brizoides*
4. *Primula florindae* Keilour hybrids
5. *Primula vialii*
6. *Arnica sachalinensis*

6

wild pots and containers

This summery confection of pastel-hued *Chaenorhinum, Diascia, Scabiosa* and *Salvia* provides a rich banquet for bees, butterflies and other pollinators. Removing faded blooms will encourage more to be produced, thereby prolonging the display.

containers for wildlife

❛ Plan individual containers for a progression of seasonal interest, so you always have something in flower, and choose plants that bloom for a long period to sustain the length of each display. ❜

Pots and containers provide valuable extra space for wild plantings of all sorts, allowing you to create mini naturalistic landscapes, even on a balcony or roof terrace. The trick is to choose appropriate plants and allow time for maintenance.

Natural effects in miniature

Whether an element of a wild garden, or the mainstay of a balcony or paved courtyard display, plantings in pots and containers can make a significant contribution to wildlife habitats. Pots offer the opportunity to experiment with planting combinations and clothe areas with flowers and foliage where growing in the ground would not be possible. They also allow you to enjoy plants that would be otherwise unsuited to your soil, such as acid-loving, ericaceous plants, including *Calluna* and camellias, in gardens with alkaline conditions.

The value of container plantings, in terms of their impact and value to wildlife, lies in the size of an individual container or the collective number of pots. Containers with a diameter of 45cm (18in) or more allow you to include large specimens, such as small trees, shrubs or climbers, or groups of perennials and annuals, creating gardens in miniature. Small pots not only hold fewer plants but also require more care because they dry out quickly, and you may become a slave to the hosepipe or watering can if you include too many.

Plan your individual containers for a progression of seasonal interest, so you always have something in flower, and choose plants that bloom for long periods to sustain the length of each display. Early spring flowers, such as hellebores and snowdrops, and autumn blooms, including salvias and dahlias, are especially valuable, as there is little other food available to pollinating insects at those times.

TOP RIGHT Be creative by upcycling ladders, chairs and other furniture to generate interesting and quirky staging for pots. This fits right in with the relaxed ambience of a wild garden.

BOTTOM RIGHT Raised beds made from natural materials, such as woven willow and hazel panels, provide the right ambience for informal drifts of shrubs and perennials.

choosing a container

AVAILABLE IN EVERY CONCEIVABLE shape, style and colour, there is a container for all gardens. The choice of materials is wide, too, and includes terracotta, ceramics, concrete, metal and plastic; a container's durability and cost depends on which type you select (see opposite). Ensure your containers have drainage holes at the bottom, or drill some, and that they are large enough for the schemes you have planned. Also consider their size and shape, which may affect the plants' long-term performance and sustainability. For example, a tall pot with a narrow base will topple easily if used for large plants, such as trees and shrubs, particularly if exposed to gusty winds. Large pots may also be unwieldy when plants need removing to refresh the compost. Avoid small-necked pots for perennials or shrubs, as they will be almost impossible to remove to repot once the vessel is filled with roots.

Repurposed pots

Recycled receptacles may also be pressed into service, and if made from natural materials, they can blend beautifully into a wild landscape. As long as they hold reasonable amounts of compost and drain freely, they will be suitable for plants. Cartons, wooden trays, orange boxes and metal drums can all be used for displays, either freestanding on the ground or hung from fences or walls. Marry durability and the suitability of reused objects with the type of plants you want to grow. Annuals will be fine in almost anything, but perennials and shrubs will require materials that don't decay quickly. Always wash recycled vessels before use and check that they didn't previously contain harmful chemicals which may damage your plants.

RIGHT Simple, understated, yet bold contrasts between plant and container can produce dramatic effects, as with this ribbed terracotta pot and sheaf of ornamental annual grasses.

TOP RIGHT Stout plastic tubs with handles enable substantial meadow-style displays to be lifted more easily, and they can also be used as liners for more decorative pots.

BOTTOM RIGHT A natural material, such as wood, makes a perfect partner for naturalistic planting schemes, but it will decay more quickly than some other materials.

SELECTING CONTAINER MATERIALS

Terracotta/clay
Ideal for rustic designs. Ensure pots are frost-proof. Containers can be heavy and fragile, and are apt to dry out in the summer.

Glazed ceramic
Wide range of colours and patterns. Pots are heavy, but tend to be more frost-proof and are less prone to drying than terracotta.

Cast and sheet metal
Good for traditional and modern schemes. Metal heats in sun and may scorch roots. Lead containers are heavy.

Stone and composites
Understated colours, ideal for 'wild' displays, these pots can be smooth or moulded. All are heavy, and real stone is expensive.

Plastic and synthetics
A broad range of colours, sizes, shapes and textures. All are lightweight and polypropylene pots are also very durable.

Recycled containers
Cheap and can lend a theatrical or amusing look. Check durability of material and ensure drainage is adequate.

COMPOST TYPES EXPLAINED

The compost required for containers is determined by the type of plants you choose and the length of time they will stay in their pot. The nutrients the plants receive also has a profound effect on their growth and performance. Use peat-free multipurpose composts for short-term plantings, such as annuals and perennials, which will be in the container for one to four years, and loam-based composts, such as John Innes types, for longer-term plants, such as shrubs and trees. Loam-based composts hold their structure longer and generally retain nutrients for longer too. But they are heavier and, as a consequence, pots will be more cumbersome to manoeuvre. Peat-free composts with added John Innes are a useful compromise. Never use garden soil for containers as it will invariably contain weed seeds and pests and diseases that could damage your plants.

Acid-loving plants, such as those growing in heathland, will need ericaceous composts that contain special blends of nutrients. Always use these for heathers, blueberries, and rhododendrons or azaleas to ensure healthy growth.

When to water

As well as selecting an appropriate compost for your potted displays (see opposite), the other important requirement is to ensure they are watered well. Whether sowing annuals from seed or growing trees and shrubs, plants in pots need a constant supply of water to maintain their vigour and health.

Germinating seed and young seedlings need to be kept moist until they have established deeper root systems, when irrigation can be reduced, watering only when the surface of the compost has dried out. However, take care not to overwater young seedlings, which can cause them to rot off or growth to become too lush.

Plugs and larger plants will need watering in until they are well established, and should be watered thereafter only when the top of the compost is dry. With annuals, trickle water gently onto the compost; powerful jets may dislodge young plants.

Food for thought

Do not feed meadow plants with fertilisers, which promote soft, sappy growth and may inhibit flower production. Most multipurpose composts contain feed for up to six weeks, sustaining shrubs, trees, bedding-type annuals and perennials. After this, use a high potash liquid feed, such as tomato fertiliser, once a month to give plants a boost. In spring, add slow release granular fertiliser to trees and shrubs in pots before they start into growth, and replenish the compost every three or four years.

OPPOSITE A late-summer arrangement of ornamental grasses, including *Pennisetum* 'Tall Tails' and *Panicum* 'Heavy Metal', with *Rudbeckia* 'Goldsturm', *Crocosmia* 'Emily McKenzie', annual *Amaranthus* , *Erigeron karvinskianus* and a mini squash.

BELOW LEFT Large containers are ideal for creating dramatic micro-meadow features, either by sowing seed mixtures of annual grasses and flowers, or planting out young plants.

BELOW TOP AND BOTTOM This half-barrel is home to a micro-meadow of durum wheat, *Triticum durum*; white laceflower, *Orlaya grandiflora*; annual *Lupinus* 'Avalune Lilac'; field poppy *Papaver rhoeas*; *Scabiosa stellata*; and cloud grass *Agrostis nebulosa*. After the flowers have faded, the seed heads of the wheat, scabious and laceflower combine in textural profusion.

planting annual micro-meadows

RIOTOUS MIXTURES of annual flowers are the quintessential feature of any wild garden and one of the cheapest ways to produce this effect is in a container. There are so many different ways to use pots, so experiment to create something new, fresh and exciting. You can use meadow-style annual seed mixes, which may include just native species or exotics, or both. Alternatively, use specific varieties or colour-themed mixtures of the same species, or mix your own. To achieve a balanced display, plan the height, spread and flowering time of your plants carefully before you begin.

Pick a perfect size

To create a micro-meadow of annuals and grasses with sufficient impact, use tubs 45cm (18in) wide or half-barrels. Smaller displays in pots can be equally effective if you select more compact, slender plant varieties.

For meadow annuals and perennials in pots, avoid composts containing fertiliser, such as multipurpose, or loam-based John Innes No 2 and 3, as they will encourage soft, sappy growth at the expense of flowers. Seed and cutting compost is the best choice, and will result in sturdier, more drought-resistant plants.

OPPOSITE An exuberant mixture of godetia flowers attracts a wide range of pollinating insects. Such displays are easily and inexpensively created and provide months of interest in any size of garden.

PLANT A POT OF ANNUAL GODETIA

Sown in late spring, this display of annual godetia, or clarkia, makes a rewarding summer feature on a patio.

SITE: Full sun
SOIL: Seed or cutting compost
MAINTENANCE NEEDED: Medium

YOU WILL NEED

- Large pot, at least 37cm (15in) in diameter
- Seed or cutting compost
- Seed mixture containing godetia or similar plants
- Seed sowing equipment (optional)
- Watering can with fine rose

PLANT CHOICES

Seed mixtures or single species, such as:
- *Clarkia* (godetia)
- *Collinsia heterophylla*
- *Eschscholzia californica* (California poppies) (above)
- *Eschscholzia lobbii*
- *Gilia*
- *Layia elegans*
- *Phacelia*

❶ SOW ONTO COMPOST
Choose a still day. Fill the container with compost, leaving a gap of 2.5–5cm (1–2in) below the pot rim. Firm to create a level surface. Sow the seed carefully and evenly over the compost.

❷ PRESS SEED DOWN
Once sown, bed the seeds in with a seed tamper or piece of wood. If you appear to have missed areas re-sow with more seed as required or wait and patch in young seedlings later.

❸ WATER WITH A ROSE

Water the seeds in with a can fitted with a fine rose. Take care not to flood the pot or use a strong spray, which may wash away the seed, resulting in patchy germination.

❹ THIN SEEDLINGS

After seedlings have germinated, transfer patches of them from over-populated areas into any gaps. If slugs prove a problem, use suitable controls. Keep seedlings moist until established.

WILDLIFE BENEFITS

- Provides pollen and nectar for a wide range of pollinating insects, especially bees and butterflies

GROWING TIPS

- Keep soil surface moist: water every few days, especially in dry or windy conditions
- Insert twigs among plants to provide support
- Remove spent blooms to encourage more to form

MAKE A POTTED MICRO-MEADOW

Bring a small slice of yesteryear into the garden with an old-fashioned corn meadow in a container.

SITE: Full sun
SOIL: Seed or cutting compost
MAINTENANCE NEEDED: Medium

YOU WILL NEED

- Large pot or half-barrel
- Seed or cutting compost
- Corn plants (if not home-grown)
- Packets of meadow-style annuals
- Twiggy stakes, if required
- Watering equipment

1 CREATE THE CORNFIELD

Fill a 60cm (2ft) tub or barrel with compost (you can first add a layer of polystyrene chips or bricks if you want to save on compost). Grow corn from seed in advance or obtain 4–6 young plants from a farmer. Plant them in the pot.

2 FILL IN THE GAPS

Leave gaps between the corn plants for other ornamental meadow plants, placing them close together to create a good display, with shorter plants around the edge. Add twiggy sticks between plants for support, if necessary.

WILDLIFE BENEFITS

- Attracts pollinating insects, particularly hoverflies, bees and butterflies
- Seeds provide food for birds and other wildlife in the autumn

3 GROWING ON

When all plants are in position, water in and keep compost moist until plants are growing well. Do not use fertiliser, as this inhibits flowering. Reduce watering after flowering when plants are going to seed.

PLANT CHOICES

- *Agrostemma githago* 'Ocean Pearl' (corncockle)
- *Ammi majus* 'Graceland' (laceflower) (above)
- *Centaurea cyanus* (cornflower)
- *Didiscus caerulea* (blue lace flower)
- *Hordeum jubatum* (squirrel grass)
- *Lamarckia aurea* (golden shower grass)
- *Papaver rhoeas* (field poppies)
- *Triticum durum* (corn plants)

GROWING TIPS

- Keep seedlings moist after germination and until established
- Keep pot watered in dry and windy periods
- Support any sagging plants at the edges of the display with twiggy sticks

LEFT AND ABOVE
Field poppy, cornflower, laceflower and white corncockle are the quintessential floral elements making up this corn meadow in a container.

DIRECT SOWING METHOD

Sowing a wildflower seed mixture around young corn plants is an effective alternative to using plug plants. Mix the seed in a bowl of dry, silver sand to bulk it up (see above). Then, using your fingers or a sieve, spread the mixture evenly around the potted corn meadow. Water in with a can fitted with a fine rose and keep the compost surface moist until seedlings establish.

WILD CONTAINER PLANTING PLANS

PLANTING IN CONTAINERS offers so much versatility and brings to life areas that may otherwise lay bare. Although they need constant attention, particularly in terms of watering, careful plant selection can play an important role in helping to create more sustainable displays.

Bowlful of prairie flowers

This shallow bowl is packed with pollinator-friendly and colourful perennials and annuals, such as the pale-hued everlasting statice, (*Limonium*) and tender *Bacopa*. The perennials can stay in position, while the annuals should be replanted each year, varying the display annually according to taste. Plant the collection in loam-based compost, such as John Innes No 1.

BOWLFUL OF PRAIRIE FLOWERS: PLANTS USED

❶ *Physostegia virginiana* 'Summer Snow' (perennial)

❷ *Coreopsis* 'Autumn Blush' (perennial)

❸ *Echinacea* 'Sunrise' (perennial)

❹ *Limonium sinuatum* (annual)

❺ *Bacopa* (annual)

High-rise containers

Awkward corners in any space are difficult to manage, but on a roof garden you have the added problems of intense sunlight and exposure to wind. These cubic aluminium planters filled with an *Amelanchier lamarckii*, grasses and seasonal flowers offer a solution. Large and lightweight, they provide plenty of room for plants' roots and they can be moved around to reflect seasonal interest.

In such an elevated position, plants of any size need to be able to withstand constant buffeting by wind. The sinuous stems of the *Amelanchier* grow through a froth of blue moor grass, which are both wind resistant, while seasonal flowers, such as tulips, violas and salvias, inject colour in pots on elevated tables. Plant in a loam-based compost, such as John Innes No 3, and water the trees and seasonal flowers regularly; the grasses and bulbs will withstand temporary drought.

HIGH-RISE CONTAINERS: PLANTS USED

❶ Tulips: 'White Triumphator'; 'Black Parrot'

❷ *Amelanchier lamarckii* (juneberry)

❸ *Sesleria nitida* (blue moor grass)

❹ Salvias and violas

naturalistic perennials and bulbs for pots

NATURALISTIC PLANTINGS OF PERENNIALS and bulbs in containers are a valuable addition to the garden and if the composition is right, they can provide displays for a number of years, often with the minimum of care. With so many species available you can create a spectrum of 'wild garden' effects, ranging from leafy ornamental grasses, such as *Stipa*, *Miscanthus* or *Panicum*, to spring woodland bulbs and prairie-style perennials. The grasses will provide diaphanous clouds or fountains of filigree flowers followed by sun-dried seed heads, while groups of carefully selected perennials will offer colourful flowers for much of the year. Try a succession of hellebores in late winter, *Pulmonaria*, *Geum* and geraniums in spring; and vibrant blasts of bright, cheerful daisies, such as *Helenium*, *Rudbeckia* and *Coreopsis*, or the richly-toned *Knautia*, *Scabiosa* and salvias, to reflect the ebullience of summer. As autumn beckons, salvias, *Agastache*, *Sedum spectabile* and *S. telephium*, asters and *Strobilanthes* will provide late colour. All are chock-full of nectar, acting as magnets for bees and butterflies.

Successful combinations

Bulbs are invaluable, too, and can be threaded through perennial schemes or simply grown on their own. Opt for single species or mixtures, or combine a succession of bulbs in one container to flower from spring through to summer. Use larger pots with sufficient space to include enough bulbs for impact. Many spring bulbs, including snowdrops, crocuses and muscari, help to feed early-foraging bees, particularly solitary and bumblebees, while early summer bulbs, such as alliums, are also good for pollinators; agapanthus and single-flowered dahlias follow with a feast for insects as winter approaches.

When combining different species and varieties, choose plants that are good natured clump-formers, whose roots will not spread too vigorously. Avoid plants such as mints (*Mentha*) and goldenrod (*Solidago*), which will soon take over and swamp neighbours. Also, only combine plants that come from the same kinds of habitat; for example, never mix moisture-loving with drought-tolerant species, or woodland with sun-loving plants, as no matter how good they may look together, your displays will inevitably struggle.

OPPOSITE As well as being attractive to wildlife, this pastel-toned arrangement of summer-flowering perennials brings a touch of elegance to a patio.

❶ SELECT THE PLANTS

Choose plants with a long season of interest and clump-forming or upright types that won't swamp their neighbours over time. Plants of different heights will help provide drama and structure. Avoid using brightly variegated flowers in naturalistic schemes.

❷ PLACE THE TALLEST

Place the largest plants in the centre or to one side of the container on a layer of multipurpose or loam-based compost. Fill around the tall plants with more compost, ensuring there is a gap of 5cm (2in) or more below the rim.

❸ FILL THE GAPS

Once the tall, anchor plants are in position, fill gaps with smaller plants, ensuring adequate compost is packed around their root balls. Adjust the position of plants if there are large gaps and avoid compressing the roots.

❹ FINAL TOUCHES

Insert the shortest, spreading plants last, allowing them to cascade over the pot rim. Water in and allow to drain, then water again so the plants settle into position. Water plants whenever the compost starts to dry out.

bijou woodlands

MANY WOODY PLANTS are quite at home in containers, providing structure and interest to areas where conventional planting may not be possible. There are trees and shrubs for all sites and situations, from full sun to shade, which are slow-growing or drought-tolerant enough for life in a pot. For sunny spots, try *Elaeagnus*, *Cercis*, bay (*Laurus nobilis*) or olive (*Olea*); in semi-shade you could use Japanese maples (*Acer japonicum*), *Viburnum*, and box (*Buxus*). Fruit trees grafted onto dwarf rootstocks are also quite easy to grow, and readily available from specialist nurseries who can advise you on varieties that are best for pots.

Other trees and shrubs for large pots are those that can be coppiced, or cut back to the ground to encourage sheaves of new shoots. Examples include *Elaeagnus*, dogwood (*Cornus*), elder (*Sambucus*), and willow (*Salix*).

Look to the sky

Many climbers can be grown in containers too. Clematis, from large-flowered hybrids to dainty *C. viticella* types and spring-flowering *C. alpina* and *C. macropetala* hybrids are options, but avoid large species, such as *C. montana*, as they will soon outgrow their pot. Honeysuckles, jasmines, passion flowers and *Trachelospermum* will also thrive in pots but will need some support (see p.54).

OPPOSITE Groups of small trees, shrubs, shade-tolerant perennials and seasonal flowers in containers can transform a gloomy patio close to a wall or fence.

MAKE A MINI WOODLAND

Containerised woodlands make fascinating and elegant features, sustaining interest over a number of years if cared for properly.

SITE: Full sun or part shade
SOIL: Loam-based compost
MAINTENANCE NEEDED: High

YOU WILL NEED

- Large pot, or half-barrel, 60cm (2ft) in diameter
- Small tree or open, sparsely-branched shrub
- Selection of shade-tolerant perennials
- Loam-based John Innes No 3 compost
- Watering equipment

PLANT CHOICES

- *Ajuga x tenorii* 'Valfredda'
- *Anemone nemorosa*
- *Athyrium nipponicum* 'Pictum'
- *Bergenia* species (above)
- *Heuchera* species
- *Malus sargentii* 'Tina'
- *Tiarella* species

① POSITION THE TREE
Choose compact trees, such as a small crab apple, with an open habit, and a pot big enough for the plants' roots. Half fill with loam-based John Innes No 3 compost. Position the tree's root ball so that there is a 5cm (2in) gap between it and the rim.

② CHOOSE SOME PERENNIALS
Almost fill the pot with compost leaving a space beneath the rim. For the area under the tree, select slow-growing, shade-tolerant evergreen perennials, such as *Ajuga*, *Tiarella*, *Heuchera*, and ferns.

❸ ADD UNDER-PLANTING

Water the perennials. Scoop out sufficient soil to insert the root ball of each plant in turn. If plants are pot-bound, carefully tease out the roots to encourage them to grow into fresh compost. Ensure plants have sufficient space to grow.

❹ KEEP WATERING

Water in plants well. Keep compost moist at all times, especially in hot, dry or windy weather. In late winter replace the top layer of compost with fresh compost, or add a slow-release fertiliser around plants.

WILDLIFE BENEFITS

- Valuable pollen and nectar for pollinating insects early in the season
- Tree berries offer food for birds in late summer or autumn

GROWING TIPS

- Keep plants watered in dry or windy weather
- Replace planting or refresh compost each spring, or add slow-release fertiliser
- Break-up or repot plantings every few years if out-growing the container

1 Sunlight illuminates the bronze foliage of *Cercis canadensis* 'Forest Pansy'.

2 Spring is enlivened with *Cercidiphyllum japonicum* f *pendulum* 'Amazing Grace' underplanted with *Muscari* bulbs.

3 Aromatic lavender makes a beautiful display on a sunny patio.

4 The autumnal flowers of *Fatsia japonica* are attractive to many insects.

5 Dwarf weeping cherries, such as *Prunus* 'Snow Fountains', make a splash with *Heuchera*, *Carex* and fescues.

6 Sweetly scented lilac, *Syringa*, offers a springtime treat for pollinators.

7 The spring-flowering cherry, *Prunus incisa* 'February Pink', with a sedge and alyssum, makes an elegant display.

wild water for small spaces

WATER GARDENING IS OFTEN CONSIDERED the preserve of larger gardens, but features in containers can form an integral part of smaller spaces too. Containers also provide flexibility, and can be emptied and moved around the garden as required.

Containers for water features should be no less than 60cm (24in) in diameter to provide room for plants; small volumes of water will also soon heat up if left in sun, which may be detrimental to both plants and wildlife. However, even features in a pot of the minimum size can make a valuable habitat for amphibians, insects and birds, particularly if access in and out of the water is provided by adjacent containers, cobbles or stones.

To create your mini wildlife pool, you can choose from large plastic tubs, ceramic urns, half-barrels or even recycled galvanised tanks or old-fashioned roll-topped baths. While ceramic and galvanised containers may be waterproof already, barrels and others may leak, so you will need to line them with a butyl pond liner or other tough plastic. The drainage holes of large ceramic pots can be plugged with rubber bungs and sealed with waterproof mastic. Some tanks may also be fitted with taps that will allow you to drain the feature easily when required.

The ideal top-up

Wherever possible, use fresh rainwater to fill the feature, rather than water from a tap, although this will suffice if nothing else is available. You can also top up levels in summer with water from a butt. Another approach is to make your potted water garden self-filling by connecting it to the downpipe of a summerhouse or shed via a water diverter. The water level can then be maintained by an overflow back to a drain or soakaway.

Choose plants carefully, avoiding those that are over vigorous, such as many British natives, as they will soon swamp the feature. Dwarf water lilies such as *Nymphaea* 'Pygmaea Rubra' or *N*. 'Pygmaea Helvola' are ideal, together with dwarf reedmace *Typha minima* or *Isolepis cernua*, which will provide a rushy effect. *Iris laevigata, Anemopsis californica* and the marsh marigold, *Caltha palustris*, will provide seasonal flowers and a snack for pollinating insects. Marginal plants can be supported on submerged bricks or slates to bring them up to their required water level, and oxygenating plants, such as *Vallisneria spiralis,* will help to keep the water in good condition.

OPPOSITE A half-barrel filled with *Iris laevigata*, yellow *Mimulus*, and *Caltha palustris* (not in flower) surrounded by pots of herbs, makes a valuable wildlife habitat.

CREATE A WILD BARREL POOL

Water gardens in large containers make fascinating features for gardens of any size.

SITE: Full sun or part shade
SOIL: Aquatic compost
MAINTENANCE NEEDED: Medium

YOU WILL NEED

- Container no less than 60cm (24in) in diameter
- Loam-based aquatic compost
- Mesh baskets for aquatic plants
- Butyl pond liner (if container is not waterproof)
- Bricks and slates for supporting plant pots
- Washed gravel for pot toppings

PLANT CHOICES

- *Anemopsis californica*
- *Caltha palustris*
- *Iris laevigata*
- *Iris sibirica*
- *Isolepis cernua*
- *Mimulus* species
- *Nymphaea* – dwarf forms
- *Typha minima* (pictured)
- *Vallisneria spiralis*

① WATERPROOF THE BARREL

Place the barrel in its final position and remove any nails or sharp objects that could puncture the liner. Open out the butyl liner, and carefully press it into the corners. Make tucks to flatten it against the sides.

② SECURE THE LINER

Once the liner is in position, attach it to the barrel wall using galvanised nails with wide flat heads, every 10–12cm (4–5in), and about 5cm (2in) from the top. Slice off surplus liner with a craft knife.

③ FILL WITH WATER

Fill the barrel with water, ideally rainwater from a butt, or via a diverter attached to a shed or summerhouse downpipe. If this isn't possible use tap water. Leave the feature overnight to ensure the liner doesn't leak.

④ INTRODUCE PLANTS

Pot up the plants in mesh baskets (see p.117) using aquatic compost. Top off pot surfaces with gravel to prevent the soil staining the water. Position the pots on bricks or tiles to the recommended water level.

WILDLIFE BENEFITS

- Pollen and nectar for pollinating insects
- Aquatic habitat for insects, invertebrates and amphibians

POOL CARE TIPS

- Water levels need topping up in summer or warm or windy weather, ideally with rainwater
- Water may need changing if it becomes stagnant
- Clean out and replant the feature every 2–3 years

7

plant gallery

annuals

For filling gaps, creating vibrant displays of colourful flowers, and providing food for a wide range of wildlife, annuals are unsurpassed. Easy to grow in most soils in sun or part shade, they start performing just a few weeks after sowing.

◑ HEIGHT		◖ SPREAD	
☼ FULL SUN		☐ DRY	
◐ PART SUN		◩ NORMAL	
✹ SHADE		◼ DAMP	

AGERATUM
◑ 0.15–0.3m (6–12in)
◖ 0.15–0.3m (6–12in)
☼ ☐

Floss flower. Half-hardy annuals and biennials, with blue, purple or white fluffy-looking flowers. A good bee and butterfly plant, use it for bedding, border edges or container displays. Sow seeds in situ in late spring or indoors in early spring.
RECOMMENDED VARIETY
A. houstonianum: blue, purple, pink and white forms available.

BORAGO OFFICINALIS
◑ 0.5–0.75m (20–30in)
◖ 0.1–0.5m (4–20in)
☼ ◐ ☐ ◩

Borage. Bristly hardy annual with heads of attractive bright blue starry flowers in summer. The blooms are magnets for bees and other pollinators, and both flowers and leaves are edible. Easy to grow in any dry soil in sun. Sow in situ in the spring or autumn. Self-seeds.
RECOMMENDED VARIETY
B. officinalis 'Alba': useful white flowered form.

CENTAUREA CYANUS
◑ 0.5–1m (20–39in)
◖ 0.1–0.5m (4–20in)
☼ ☐ ◩

Cornflower. Slender hardy annual, the branching stems are topped by colourful flowers, often double, from summer to autumn. Useful for seed mixtures, gaps in borders or pots. Good for pollinators. Sow in situ in spring or autumn.
RECOMMENDED VARIETIES
C. c. 'Black Ball': purple flowers; 'White Ball': white form; 'Blue Diadem': ruffled blue flowers.

CERINTHE MAJOR 'PURPURASCENS'
◑ 0.5–1m (20–39in)
◖ 0.1–0.5m (4-20in)
☼ ☐ ◩

Distinctive hardy annual, with purple flowers and bracts on curved stems covered in glaucous foliage. The spring to early summer flowers are loved by bees and butterflies. Sow in spring or late summer in situ or in pots indoors in early spring. Gently self–seeds.

CLARKIA
◑ 0.5–1m (20–39in)
◖ 0.1–0.5m (4–20in)
☼ ◐ ☐

Godetia. Erect, bushy hardy annual plants with pink, purple or white flowers in early summer. The petals are often lobed. Good for pollinators, but choose single-flowered forms. Sow in situ in spring or indoors in pots or trays in early spring.
RECOMMENDED VARIETY
Clarkia amoena: upright annual with bowl-shaped flowers, often multicoloured.

COSMOS BIPINNATUS
◑ 0.3–2.5 m (1–8ft)
◖ 0.1–0.5m (4–20in)
☼ ☐ ◩

Upright, with branching habit and feathery foliage. Long-lasting daisy flowers in red, pink, purple, white or yellow appear from midsummer to first frosts. Late food source for bees and butterflies. Sow in situ in spring or in trays or pots indoors.
RECOMMENDED VARIETIES
C. 'Antiquity': faded pink flowers; 'Purity': white flowers; 'Rubenza': dusky red flowers; 'Sonata Series': dwarf form.

ESCHSCHOLZIA
◑ 0.3–0.5m (12–20in)
◖ 0.2–0.5m (8–20in)
☼ ☐ ◩

California poppy. Rewarding, long-flowered annual in sensational range of colours, with blue-green dissected foliage. Attractive to bees. Sow in situ in spring and autumn. Easy to grow in free-draining soil, it is drought-tolerant and will self-seed.
RECOMMENDED VARIETIES
E. 'Butter Bush': pale yellow flowers; 'Ivory Castle': creamy white flowers; 'Red Chief': scarlet flowers.

HELIANTHUS ANNUUS
○ 1–1.5m (39in–5ft)
⊃ 0.2–0.5 m (8–20in)
☼ □

Sunflower. Quick-growing annual, either with a single stout stem or branched habit. Large yellow, white or rustic-toned daisy flowers appear in summer. Good for pollinators and seeds loved by birds. Sow in situ or indoors in spring.

RECOMMENDED VARIETIES
H. a. 'Russian Giant': large yellow heads; 'Autumn Beauty': multicoloured heads.

LIMNANTHES DOUGLASII
○ 0.15m (6in)
⊃ 0.15m+ (6in+)
☼ □ ▭

Poached egg plant. Low-growing, with yellow and white flowers in early summer. Good for edging beds and paths. Valuable for pollinators, such as bees and hoverflies. Sow in situ in spring or autumn; it will self-seed freely.

RECOMMENDED VARIETIES
L. d. subsp *sulphurea*: pure yellow flowers; *L. d.* subsp *nivea*: white flowers.

LOBULARIA MARITIMA
○ 0.1m (4in)
⊃ 0.25m (10in)
☼ □ ▭

Sweet alyssum. Spreading hardy annual with grey–green narrow leaves. Round heads of sweetly scented flowers that are good for pollinators appear in summer and early autumn. Ideal for border and path edges, and pots. Sow seed in situ in spring.

RECOMMENDED VARIETY
L. m. 'Snow Crystals': pure white flowers.

MYOSOTIS SYLVATICA
○ 0.1–0.3m (4–12in)
⊃ 0.1–0.5m (4–20in)
☼ ◑ ▭

Forget-me-not. Low growing late spring-flowering plants, often used as annual bedding, but really a biennial sown the previous year. Use for path or border edges, or with bulbs. Sow in pots in early summer and plant out in autumn or spring. Self-seeds.

RECOMMENDED VARIETIES
M. 'Royal Blue': rich blue form; 'Snowsylva': white flowers.

NICOTIANA
○ 0.3–1.5m (1–5ft)
⊃ 0.1–0.5m (4–20in)
☼ ◑ ▭

Tobacco plant. Half-hardy annuals or perennials, usually grown as annuals. Leafy plants with tubular, sweetly scented flowers, in a wide range of colours. The blooms often open at night and are attractive to moths. Sow in spring indoors, and plant outside after frosts.

RECOMMENDED VARIETY
N. alata 'Grandiflora': white flowers, highly scented at night.

PAPAVER RHOEAS
○ 0.5–0.9m (20–36in)
⊃ 0.3m (12in)
☼ ◑ □ ▭

Field poppy. Familiar hardy British native found in field margins, road verges and disturbed soil. Scarlet flowers appear from early to late summer. Ideal for borders, annual meadow mixes and open grassland. Valuable for pollinators. Sow in situ in autumn or spring. Easy to grow, it will self-seed.

RECOMMENDED VARIETY
P. 'Shirley Mixed' : pastel, multicoloured flowers.

PHACELIA
○ 0.15–0.3m (6–12in)
⊃ 0.3m (12in)
☼ ◑ □

Desert bluebell. Fast growing feathery or round-leaved hardy annuals with masses of small bright blue cup-shaped flowers from early summer. Makes good edging for paths or borders with poor, dryish soils. The blooms are valuable for many kinds of pollinator. Sow seed outdoors in situ in spring or autumn.

RECOMMENDED VARIETY
P. tanacetifolia: feathery-leaved, mid-blue flowers.

ZINNIA
○ 0.3–0.5 (12–20in)
⊃ 0.2–0.5m (8–20in)
☼

Distinctive half-hardy annual, with daisy-like flowers in a wide range of colours, except blue. Flowering from late summer into autumn, it provides a valuable late source of nectar. Needs warmth and shelter. Sow in spring indoors or in situ in late spring after the frosts.

RECOMMENDED VARIETIES
Z. Zahara Series: bushy plants in a range of vivid colours, often two-toned.

biennials & perennials

Easy to grow, perennials are the mainstay of the flower garden, providing food for pollinators while their foliage offers cover for other wildlife. Most die back during the winter but a few are evergreen. Biennials grow leaves in their first year and bloom in the second, but often self-seed when happy.

- ⬤ HEIGHT ⬌ SPREAD
- ☼ FULL SUN ☐ DRY
- ◑ PART SUN ◪ NORMAL
- ✴ SHADE ■ DAMP

ACHILLEA
- ⬤ 0.5–2.5m (20in–8ft)
- ⬌ 0.2–1m (8–39in)
- ☼ ☐ ◪

Upright hardy perennials with dark green to grey feathered aromatic leaves. Flat-topped flower heads in many colours, appear in summer, often changing tone with age. Lift and divide every 3–4 years, or take cuttings.

RECOMMENDED VARIETY
A. filipendulina 'Gold Plate': tall plants with flat-topped golden-yellow flowers.

ANCHUSA AZUREA
- ⬤ 0.5–1m (20–39in)
- ⬌ 0.2m (8in)
- ☼ ◑ ☐ ◪

Upright hardy perennial with narrow, bristly leaves. Rich blue flowers, attractive to bees and other pollinators, bloom in early summer. Deadhead to encourage further flowering. It is ideal for borders and naturalistic settings.

RECOMMENDED VARIETY
A. a. 'Loddon Royalist': a tall variety, with deep blue edible flowers.

ASTER AND SYMPHYOTRICHUM
- ⬤ 0.4–2.5m (16in–8ft)
- ⬌ 0.4–1.8m (16in–6ft)
- ☼ ◑ ◪ ■

Mound-forming to upright perennials, bearing masses of daisy flowers in a variety of colours, notably pink and mauve, from summer. Late performers offer valuable food for pollinators. Ideal for borders or naturalistic designs.

RECOMMENDED VARIETY
S. 'Little Carlow': hip-height form with violet-blue daisies from late summer.

ASTRANTIA MAJOR
- ⬤ 0.5–1m (20–39in)
- ⬌ 0.2–0.5m (8–20in)
- ☼ ◑ ◪ ■

Hattie's pincushion. Useful perennials, with long-lasting pincushion-like flowers in summer. The flower bracts are green, cream to deep maroon red, and the blooms attract bees and pollinating flies. Ideal for woodland edges and borders that are not too dry. The foliage is slug resistant.

RECOMMENDED VARIETY
A. m. 'Roma': tall, long-flowering variety with large silver and pink blooms.

AQUILEGIA
- ⬤ 0.3–1m (12–39in)
- ⬌ 0.1–0.5m (4–20in)
- ☼ ◑ ☐ ◪

Columbine. Graceful, clump-forming, short-lived perennial with ferny foliage. Nodding, bell-shaped spurred flowers appear in spring and summer in a wide range of colours and shapes. A good bee plant, it is easy to grow and some species naturalise readily.

RECOMMENDED VARIETY
A. vulgaris: a tall species, Granny-bonnets come in wide range of flower colours and shapes.

CENTAUREA
- ⬤ 0.5–1m (20–39in)
- ⬌ 0.1–0.5m (4–20in)
- ☼ ◑ ☐ ◪

Knapweed. Range of hardy perennials with tufted thistle-like flowers, attractive to pollinators, in shades of blue, pink, yellow, white and red, The blooms appear for many weeks from late spring, and are followed by attractive seed heads. Tolerant of drought and poor soil.

RECOMMENDED VARIETY
C. montana: compact species; blue, white, pink or purple flowers in late spring.

CENTRANTHUS RUBER
- ⬤ 0.5–1m (20–39in)
- ⬌ 0.2–0.5m (8–20in)
- ☼ ☐

Red valerian. Semi-evergreen perennial with a woody rootstock. Heads of tightly packed tiny pink or white musky-scented flowers appear in summer. Highly attractive to pollinators, such as bees and butterflies. Drought tolerant, it self-seeds, but may become invasive.

RECOMMENDED VARIETIES
C. r. 'Coccineus': deep pink flowers; 'Albus': white flowers.

DIANTHUS
⬆ 0.1–1m (4–39in)
⬇ 0.1–0.5m (4–20in)
☼ ☐

Pinks. Evergreen perennials or biennials with silvery-blue or bright green foliage. Pink, red or white flowers, often intricately marked and scented, form in summer often on tall, thin stems. The blooms attract bees and butterflies.

RECOMMENDED VARIETY
D. carthusianorum: grassy foliage and magenta flowers from late summer.

DIGITALIS
⬆ 0.6–2.5m (2–8ft)
⬇ 0.6m (2ft)
☼ ◑ ✱ ☐ ▭ ■

Foxglove. Distinctive range of biennials and short-lived perennials with tall spires of long-lasting tubular flowers in white, pink, yellow or rusty bronze tones. Attractive to bees and butterflies. Bronze-toned species prefer sun, grow others in sun or shade.

RECOMMENDED VARIETY
D. purpurea 'Alba': tall, white-flowered variant.

ECHINOPS
⬆ 0.5–1.5m (20in–5ft)
⬇ 0.3–1m (12–39in)
☼ ◑ ☐

Globe thistle. Tall perennials, with spiny, grey-green leaves. Silvery-blue or white globe-shaped spiky flowers appear in summer and persist for many months. Ideal for poor soils in full sun, they attract many pollinators and also make good cut flowers.

RECOMMENDED VARIETY
E. ritro 'Veitch's Blue': waist height with rich blue flowers.

ECHIUM VULGARE
⬆ 0.8–1m (30–39in)
⬇ 0.1–0.5m (4–20in)
☼ ☐ ▭

Viper's bugloss. A biennial, with a rosette of bristly leaves in the first year, and long-lasting spikes of vivid blue flowers the following year. An important food plant for pollinating insects. It self-seeds in well-drained soil and sun.

RECOMMENDED VARIETY
E. v. 'Blue Bedder': dwarf, compact form of the species, reaching just 0.45m (18in).

ERYNGIUM
⬆ 0.4–2.5 m (15in–8ft)
⬇ 0.2–1.5m (8in–5ft)
☼ ☐ ▭

Sea holly. Clump-forming or erect thistle-like biennials, or, more commonly, perennials with green or silvery leaves and striking, long-lasting silver or blue spiky flowers. Attractive to bees, pollinating wasps and hoverflies. Grow sea hollies in borders, naturalistic plantings or gravel.

RECOMMENDED VARIETY
E. x zabelii 'Violetta': medium height, with deep blue flowers in late summer.

EUPATORIUM
⬆ 1–1.5m (3ft 3in–5ft)
⬇ 1–1.5m (3ft 3in–5ft)
☼ ◑ ▭ ■

Hemp. Stout, upright, architectural perennials for damp soils. Flat heads of dusky pink or white flowers are produced from midsummer and offer late nectar for bees and butterflies. Ideal for borders, naturalistic plantings, bog gardens or pond margins.

RECOMMENDED VARIETY
E. cannabinum: tall European native, with tufted pinky–purple flowers in summer.

EUPHORBIA
⬆ 0.1–1.5m (4in–5ft)
⬇ 0.1–1.5m (4in–5ft)
☼ ◑ ✱ ☐ ▭

Spurge. Deciduous or evergreen perennials with flower heads composed of yellow bracts. Grown for their bold foliage and sculptural qualities, deciduous species also offer autumn colour. Best for borders, naturalistic plantings, gravel and coastal gardens. Sap is a skin irritant.

RECOMMENDED VARIETY
E. characias: tall evergreen species with yellow flowers in spring; has many varieties.

GALIUM ODORATUM
⬆ 0.15–0.3m (6–12in)
⬇ 1–1.5m+ (39in–5ft +)
☼ ◑ ✱ ▭ ■

Sweet woodruff. Vigorous, carpeting woodland plant, with small aromatic whorls of leaves. The sweetly scented, star-shaped white flowers, which appear from late spring, are attractive to bees and other pollinators. It makes good ground cover in shady areas, or in sunnier positions if the soil is not too dry. Trim off dead foliage in late winter.

GAURA LINDHEIMERI
- 1–1.5m (39in–5ft)
- 0.3–0.5m (12–20in)

Perennial, often short-lived or grown as an annual in cold climates. It forms clumps of long, thin, wand-like stems with narrow leaves covered in airy white to deep pink flowers over a long period in summer. Good for pollinators, it needs full sun to thrive.

RECOMMENDED VARIETY

G. l. 'Siskiyou Pink': bright pink long-lasting flowers.

GERANIUM
- 0.2–1.2m (8in–4ft)
- 0.15–1.2m (6in–4ft)

Clump-forming to spreading perennials; some are semi-evergreen. They flower from spring to autumn, depending on species, and all are good for pollinators. Ideal ground cover, even beneath trees. Trim after main flowering to refresh foliage and blooms.

RECOMMENDED VARIETY

G. macrorrhizum: pink, white or mauve flowers in summer.

HELENIUM
- 0.5–1.2m (20in–4ft)
- 0.15–1m (6–39in)

Sneezeweed. Valuable late summer and autumn-flowering perennials, with long-lasting daisy-like blooms in vibrant tones, including red, yellow, orange and bronze. Good food source for pollinators. Ideal for borders or naturalistic planting schemes.

RECOMMENDED VARIETY

H. autumnale: late-summer red, yellow or orange flowers.

HELLEBORUS
- 0.3–0.5m (12–20in)
- 0.3–0.5m (12–20in)

Valuable winter-flowering perennials, some evergreen, others herbaceous. Most are ideal for semi-shaded situations; grow evergreen *H. argutifolius* in sun. Wide range of flower colours available; some forms will self-seed.

RECOMMENDED VARIETY

H. x hybridus: Lenten rose. Semi-evergreen species, early spring flowers in many colours.

HESPERIS MATRONALIS
- 0.5–1.2m (20in–4ft)
- 0.3–0.5 m (12–20in)

Sweet rocket. Short-lived perennial with sweetly-scented lilac flowers that appear from late spring. A good plant for pollinators, ideally grow it in moist soil in full sun, where it will self-seed and naturalise in borders, naturalistic plantings, pond margins and open grassland.

RECOMMENDED VARIETY

H. m. var *albiflora*: an attractive white-flowered form of the species.

KNAUTIA MACEDONICA
- 0.5–1m (20–39in)
- 0.3–0.5m (12–20in)

Crimson scabious. An easy-to-grow perennial, but it can be short-lived if not happy where it is growing. Heads of ruby-red flowers on long, airy stems appear from summer to early autumn. It attracts many pollinators, especially butterflies, and prefers chalky soil that is not too dry.

RECOMMENDED VARIETY

K. m. 'Mars Midget': shorter, sturdier selection of the species.

LAMIUM
- 0.1–0.5 m (4–20in)
- 0.1–1m (4–39in)

Deadnettle. Spreading semi-evergreen perennials. Upright shoots of dusky-red, pink or white hooded flowers appear from spring to summer; some have silver or marbled foliage. Valuable for bees and other pollinators, it is ideal for dry, shady positions.

RECOMMENDED VARIETY

L. maculatum 'White Nancy': silvery foliage and spikes of yellow flowers in summer.

LEUCANTHEMUM VULGARE
- 0.5–1m (20–39in)
- 0.1–0.5m (4–20in)

Ox–eye daisy. Semi–evergreen spreading perennial with an open, upright habit. White, yellow–centred daisies appear over a long period from spring onwards. A valuable pollinator plant, and important constituent of seed mixtures, it can also be grown on its own. Sow seed in situ in spring or autumn, or plant plugs in the spring.

LIATRIS SPICATA
0.5–0.9m (20–36in)
0.2–0.45m (8–18in)

Gay feather. Clump forming perennials with narrow leaves. Spires of long-lasting bottle-brush flowers appear from midsummer to autumn, in pink, purple and white. Valuable for bees and butterflies, use it for naturalistic plantings.

RECOMMENDED VARIETY
L. s. 'Kobold': magenta flowers complemented by fresh green foliage.

LYTHRUM
0.5–1.5m (20in–5ft)
0.2–0.5m (8–20in)

Loosestrife. Clump-forming perennials with flower spikes in shades of pink or white from early summer. Good for pond margins or borders with moist soil. The blooms attract bees and butterflies, but it self-seeds and can be invasive.

RECOMMENDED VARIETY
L. salicaria: selections of this British native come in various shades of pink, such as 'Blush'.

MALVA MOSCHATA
0.5–1m (20–39in)
0.3–1m (12–39in)

Musk mallow. Tall perennial inhabiting field margins, hedgerows and wasteland. Pale pink flowers appear in summer and are attractive to many pollinators. Grow in borders or in grass. Sow seed in situ in spring or autumn.

RECOMMENDED VARIETY
M. m. 'Alba': elegant white form, effective among many border perennials.

MONARDA DIDYMA
0.5–1m (20–39in)
0.3–0.5m (12–20in)

Bergamot. Upright, clump-forming perennials, with oval, aromatic leaves. Whorls of hooded, red, pink, purple or white flowers, attractive to bees, appear in summer. Buy mildew-resistant varieties, especially for rich soils. Best for borders or naturalistic designs.

RECOMMENDED VARIETY
M. 'Violet Queen': mildew resistant; purple-pink flowers.

NEPETA
0.6–0.9m (24–36in)
0.3–0.5m (12–20in)

Catmint. Spreading perennials with small, aromatic, grey-green leaves. Massed spires of small blue hooded flowers are produced over a long period in summer. Very attractive to many pollinators, including bees, and cats! Good for informal drifts, larger border edgings or gravel gardens.

RECOMMENDED VARIETY
N. racemosa 'Walker's Low': compact form with violet flowers. Clip after flowering.

ORIGANUM VULGARE
0.2–0.6m (8–24in)
0.3–0.5m (12–20in)

Pot marjoram. Mat-forming to small shrubby perennials with aromatic leaves. Clusters of blue, white or pink flowers are formed on short stems in summer. A valuable plant for many pollinators, it is ideal for border or path edges, gravel gardens, or pots.

RECOMMENDED VARIETY
O. vulgare 'Compactum': low-growing, compact variety of the British native species.

PAPAVER
0.2–1m (8–39in)
0.1–0.3m (4–12in)

Poppy. Includes a wide range of biennials and perennials, often short-lived. Cup-shaped 'poppy' flowers in many colours, except blue, appear in summer. Bumblebees adore them. Most prefer full sun, and they will self-seed and naturalise in free-draining and poor soils.

RECOMMENDED VARIETY
P. orientale: the tall perennial oriental poppy has colourful flowers from late spring.

PENSTEMON
0.3–1m (12–39in)
0.2–0.3m (8–12in)

Shrubby evergreen or semi-evergreen perennials, sometimes short-lived. They bear spikes of snapdragon-like flowers, loved by bees, in many colours from mid-summer. Ideal for borders, gravel, and path edges in moist but well-drained soil. Some are not very hardy.

RECOMMENDED VARIETY
P. heterophyllus 'Heavenly Blue': semi-evergreen and hardy, with bright blue flowers.

PERSICARIA
♠ 0.1–1.5m (4in–5ft)
➲ 0.1–1.5m (4in–5ft)
☼ ◐ ▢ ■
Bistort. Mat to clump-forming herbaceous or evergreen perennials, often with attractive, blotched foliage. Red, pink or white flower spires appear from summer. Plants prefer moist soil and pond margins. Some are invasive.
RECOMMENDED VARIETY
P. amplexicaule: tall species with spear-shaped leaves and red late-summer flowers.

PHLOMIS
♠ 0.5–1.5m (20in–5ft)
➲ 0.3–1.5m (12in–5ft)
☼ ▢ ▢
Herbaceous or evergreen perennials, some with felted leaves. Spires of whorled yellow or pink summer blooms are followed by attractive seed heads. Good for many pollinators, especially bees. Grow in borders or gravel.
RECOMMENDED VARIETY
P. russeliana: tall species with felted leaves and long-lasting soft yellow hooded flowers.

POLEMONIUM CAERULEUM
♠ 0.4–1m (16–39in)
➲ 0.3–0.5m (12–20in)
☼ ◐ ▢ ■
Jacob's ladder. Erect perennial, often short lived. The foliage's leaflets resemble ladders. Flowers in blue, mauve or white appear from late spring and are valuable for bees. Self-seeds and naturalises in moist soil.
RECOMMENDED VARIETY
P. c. 'Bambino Blue': short, blue compact version of the species.

PRIMULA VULGARIS AND PRIMULA VERIS
♠ 0.1–0.5 m (4–20in)
➲ 0.1–0.3m (4–12in)
☼ ◐ ▢ ■
Primrose/cowslip. Semi-evergreen or herbaceous and spring-flowering, primroses have pale yellow flowers on short stalks; cowslips (*P. veris*) bear clusters of bell-shaped yellow blooms on taller stems. Grow primroses in semi-shade or sun in moist but well-drained soil; cowslips prefer damper conditions. Both self-seed.

PRUNELLA VULGARIS
♠ 0.05–0.3m (2–12in)
➲ 0.1–0.5m (4–20in)
☼ ◐ ▢ ▢ ■
Self-heal. Semi-evergreen creeping perennial that roots as it spreads. Oval leaves and short spikes of hooded blue flowers, loved by bees and other pollinators, appear in summer and autumn. Often found in neglected lawns, it can withstand being mown. Grows well in many soil types. Establish from seed, plugs or plantlets. Will naturalise, but can be invasive.

PULMONARIA
♠ 0.3m (12in)
➲ 0.45m (18in)
☼ ◐ ▢ ▢
Lungwort. Clump-forming perennials with attractive spear-shaped, often spotted or silvery, leaves. Small heads of bell-shaped, long-lasting flowers in blue, red, pink, purple or white appear from early spring. Ideal beneath trees or shrubs, it is a great bee plant. New foliage produced in autumn remains over winter.
RECOMMENDED VARIETIES
P. 'Silver Bouquet': pink/blue flowers, silvery leaves.

SALVIA
♠ 0.3–2.5m (1–8ft)
➲ 0.3–1.2m (1–4ft)
☼ ▢ ▢
Sage. Clump-forming herbaceous to evergreen, upright to mound-forming perennials with aromatic foliage. Spires of hooded flowers in many colours, often vibrant, appear from midsummer and attract many pollinators. Best in moist, but well-drained to dry soil. Many are drought tolerant.
RECOMMENDED VARIETY
S. nemorosa: knee-height with blue, white or pink flowers.

SANGUISORBA
♠ 1–2.5m (39in–8ft)
➲ 0.3–1m (12–39in)
☼ ◐ ▢ ■
Burnet. Wiry perennials with airy, rounded leaflets. Long-lasting bobble or tasselled flowers on long stems in dark red, pink and white appear from summer into autumn. Best for borders and naturalistic plantings in moist but not wet soils.
RECOMMENDED VARIETY
S. officinalis 'Tanna': hip-height form, with maroon-red bobble-headed flowers throughout summer.

RUDBECKIA

🔆 0.6–1.8m (2–6ft)
🔄 0.3–1.8m (1–6ft)
☼ ◐ ☐ ▭

Cone flower/black-eyed
Susan. Clump-forming
perennials (and annuals) that
produce long-lasting yellow
or dusky-toned daisy flowers
with prominent dark central
cones from summer to
autumn. Good for pollinators.

RECOMMENDED VARIETY
R. fulgida var sullivantii
'Goldsturm': short form
with yellow flowers.

SCABIOSA
🌢 0.2–0.7m (8–28in)
🌢 0.2–0.5m (8–20in)
☼ ◐ ☐ ▣

Scabious. Clump-forming perennials with dissected leaves. Held on wiry stems, the disc-shaped summer flowers come in many colours and are attractive to pollinators. Plant in beds, naturalistic plantings or pots in well-drained soil.

RECOMMENDED VARIETY
S. columbaria subsp *ochroleuca*: tall form with pale yellow flowers in late summer.

SEDUM
🌢 0.05–0.5m (2–20in)
🌢 0.2–0.5m (8–20in)
☼ ◐ ☐ ▣

Upright or mat-forming perennials, with deciduous to evergreen succulent leaves. Flat flower heads in pink, white, red, or yellow form in late summer and autumn. Good for pollinators, they are drought tolerant. Plant in beds, gravel gardens or coastal sites.

RECOMMENDED VARIETY
S. spectabile: upright form, with pink, white or red flowers.

SILENE
🌢 0.3–1m (12–39in)
🌢 0.2–0.4m (8–16in)
☼ ◐ ☐ ▣

Campion. Deciduous or evergreen perennials with rounded flowers on tubes in red, pink or white. Some are British natives, and all are good for pollinators. Mat-forming types are ideal for gravel or edging; use upright forms for borders or naturalising.

RECOMMENDED VARIETY
S.dioica: red campion; pink early-summer flowers.

SOLIDAGO
🌢 0.4–2.1m (16in–7ft)
🌢 0.45–1.8m (18in–6ft)
☼ ☐ ▣ ■

Goldenrod. Upright perennials with sprays of golden flowers from late summer into autumn. They provide valuable food for many pollinators. Many species are invasive – use compact forms in small gardens – but good for large beds and naturalistic designs.

RECOMMENDED VARIETY
S. 'Little Lemon': dwarf form with yellow flowers in summer.

STACHYS
🌢 0.1–0.5m (4–20in)
🌢 0.2–1m (8–39in)
☼ ◐ ☐ ▣

The green or felted leaves of these herbaceous or semi-evergreen perennials are joined in summer by spikes of pink or white flowers. Reliable and long-lived, the blooms are very attractive to bees. Good for border edgings and naturalistic plantings. They thrive in well-drained soils.

RECOMMENDED VARIETY
S. officinalis 'Rosa Superba': rose-pink flowers in summer.
S. byzantina: soft silver foliage.

VERBASCUM
🌢 0.5–1m (20–39in)
🌢 0.3–1m (12–39in)
☼ ☐ ▣

Mullein. Biennial or short-lived perennials, often forming large rosettes of basal leaves, sometimes adorned with silky hairs. Spires studded with flowers in all shades, except pure blue, appear in summer, and are good for pollinators. Plants will naturalise from seed in poor, well-drained soils.

RECOMMENDED VARIETY
V. thapsus: British native with rosettes of hairy grey leaves, and spires of yellow flowers.

VERBENA BONARIENSIS
🌢 1.5–2.5m (5–8ft)
🌢 0.2–0.5m (8–20in)
☼ ☐ ▣

Tall, wiry, loosely spreading perennial with airy, branching heads of purple-blue flowers from summer to autumn. A good late food source for pollinators, it is tender in cold climates, but easy to grow from seed. Ideal for borders or naturalistic plantings, it grows well in poor soils.

RECOMMENDED VARIETY
V. b. 'Lollipop': dwarf compact form reaches about 0.6m (24in) in height.

VERONICA
🌢 0.1–1.5m (4in–5ft)
🌢 0.1–1m (4–39in)
☼ ◐ ☐ ▣

Mat-forming to upright herbaceous or evergreen perennials, with spires of small summer flowers that are attractive to pollinators, in shades of blue, red, pink, purple and white. Useful for borders, path edges and naturalistic planting schemes.

RECOMMENDED VARIETY
V. longifolia 'Marietta': mid-height, long-flowered variety with dark blue flowers. Mildew resistant.

grasses, sedges & rushes

This invaluable and highly diverse group of plants is indispensable for naturalistic or meadow-style planting designs. Grown for their foliage, flowers, and, in many cases, their autumn colour, there are grasses and grass-like plants suitable for all sites and situations.

- ⋂ HEIGHT
- ☼ FULL SUN
- ☀ PART SUN
- ✲ SHADE
- ⊃ SPREAD
- ☐ DRY
- ▭ NORMAL
- ■ DAMP

ARUNDO
⋂ 1.5–8m (5–26ft)
⊃ 0.5–1.5m (20in–5ft)
☼ ☐ ▭

Giant reed. Stout, evergreen grass with tall stems. Not fully hardy in colder climates, but can be invasive in warmer gardens. Good for the back of a larger border, gravel or Mediterranean gardens, or large containers. Plants like moist, well-drained soil.
RECOMMENDED VARIETY
A. donax 'Macrophylla': wide blue-green leaves.

CALAMAGROSTIS x ACUTIFLORA
⋂ 1–1.5m (39in–5ft)
⊃ 0.5–1m (20–39in)
☼ ☀ ☐ ▭

Feather reed grass. Tall, upright deciduous grass with buff plume-like flowers from late summer. It creates a good winter silhouette; use it as a bold accent in borders or naturalistic plantings. Best in moist, well-drained soil.
RECOMMENDED VARIETY
C. x a. 'Karl Foerster': bold, upright form.

CAREX
⋂ 0.1–1.5m (4in–5ft)
⊃ 0.1–1.5m (4in–5ft)
☼ ☀ ▭ ■

Sedge. Mostly evergreen, tussock-forming to spreading perennials. Decorative leaves in blue-green, brown and ochre tones, the flowers and seed heads are also pretty. Good for naturalistic, gravel, coastal or bog gardens, depending on species.
RECOMMENDED VARIETY
C. buchananii: arching brown, evergreen foliage.

CYPERUS LONGUS
⋂ 1.5–2m (5–6ft 8in)
⊃ 0.5–1m (20–39in)
☼ ☀ ■

Sweet galingale. Vigorous, upright semi-evergreen, moisture-loving perennial. Although hardy, the spoke-like foliage lends a tropical or architectural air. Reddish-brown flower spikes form in summer. Ideal for a pond-side or boggy ground, it spreads via underground runners and can be invasive in small spaces unless constrained.

DESCHAMPSIA CESPITOSA
⋂ 0.5–1.5m (20in–5ft)
⊃ 0.3–1m (12–39in)
☼ ☀ ☐ ▭

Hair grass. Tussock-forming semi-evergreen perennial, grown for its clouds of 'see-through' flowers, which appear in summer but persist into autumn. Effective as specimens, or in borders or naturalistic schemes, in moist, well-drained soils.
RECOMMENDED VARIETY
D. c. 'Bronzeschleier': filamentous clouds of bronzed flowers that age to beige.

FESTUCA
⋂ 0.1–1m (4–39in)
⊃ 0.1–0.5m (4–20in)
☼ ☐ ▭

Fescue. Tussock or mat-forming grasses, mostly evergreen, but some are deciduous. Filamentous leaves, often in striking colours, such as blue, bright green, or yellow, with attractive flower heads. Best for border edges, gravel and naturalistic plantings in well-drained soil.
RECOMMENDED VARIETY
F. amethystina: tussocks of green foliage, with airy flower heads from summer.

HAKONECHLOA MACRA
⋂ 0.3–0.5m (12–20in)
⊃ 0.3–0.5m (12–20in)
☀ ▭

Hakone grass. Deciduous gently-spreading, broad-leaved grass with elegant arching habit. The flowers are insignificant. It needs damp soil and part shade to thrive. Grow along path edges or in informal drifts, or in containers. Trim off brown foliage in spring.
RECOMMENDED VARIETY
H. m. 'Nicholas': the green leaves develop red tones in the autumn.

LUZULA
♦ 0.3–0.6m (12–24in)
⊃ 0.3–0.6m (12–24in)
☼ ◑ ✹ ☐ ▢ ■

Woodrush. Creeping evergreen rosettes form spreading mats of grassy foliage. Heads of small brown or white flowers have a subtle charm from spring. Thrives in full shade and dry conditions under trees. Useful for ground cover and naturalising.

RECOMMENDED VARIETY
L. nivea: deep green leaves and white flowers in summer.

MISCANTHUS SINENSIS
♦ 0.5–2.5m (20in–8ft)
⊃ 0.2–1.5m (8in–5ft)
☼ ☐ ▢ ■

Eulalia grass. Deciduous, clump-forming species with many varieties. Cultivars offer attractive foliage, long-lasting flowers and upright habit. Grow in moist, well-drained soil in borders and naturalistic plantings, or large containers.

RECOMMENDED VARIETY
M. s. 'Flamingo': leaves with white midrib; late-summer flowers are tinged pink.

MOLINIA CAERULEA
♦ 0.7–1.8m (28in–6ft)
⊃ 0.7–1m (28–39in)
☼ ◑ ☐ ▢

Purple moor grass. Clump-forming species adaptable to any moist, well-drained soil. Many selections, grown for their foliage, flowers and autumn tints. Use in pots, beds or naturalistic plantings.

RECOMMENDED VARIETY
M. c. subsp *arundinacea* 'Windspiel': Tall form with airy seed heads and honey-coloured autumn tints.

PANICUM VIRGATUM
♦ 0.5–1m (20–39in)
⊃ 0.5–1m (20–39in)
☼ ☐ ▢

Switch grass. Clump-forming upright deciduous perennial, with airy, long-lasting flowers and seed heads. Reliable autumn tints and winter skeletons. Grow in borders or naturalistic schemes with flowering perennials, in moist to well-drained soil.

RECOMMENDED VARIETY
P. v. 'Shenandoah': leaves turn burgundy in autumn.

PENNISETUM
♦ 0.4–1.5m (16in–5ft)
⊃ 0.4–1.5m (16in–5ft)
☼ ☐ ▢

Fountain grass. Clump-forming deciduous to evergreen perennials, some short-lived. Habits vary from compact tussocks to upright clumps, but all produce long-lasting bottle-brush flowers in late summer. Grow in borders or large pots in well-drained soil. Some species are slightly tender.

RECOMMENDED VARIETY
P. alopecuroides 'Hameln': deciduous, with tall flower stems above a compact base.

POA LABILLARDIEREI
♦ 0.9m–1.2m (36in–4ft)
⊃ 0.9–1m (36–39in)
☼ ☐ ▢

New Zealand blue grass. Semi-evergreen tussock-forming grass with filamentous blue-green foliage and silvery-blue seed heads in summer. Good for the middle of the border and drifts in naturalistic plantings among other perennials. Grow in moist, well-drained soil, and comb out old leaves in spring to maintain a fresh appearance.

STIPA
♦ 0.5–2.5m (20in–8ft)
⊃ 0.1–1m (4–39in)
☼ ☐ ▢

Feather grass. Clump-forming deciduous to evergreen perennials, with long-lasting ornamental flower and seed heads, often filamentous or plume-like. Ideal for borders, naturalistic plantings, gravel gardens and pots, grow them in moist to well-drained soil.

RECOMMENDED VARIETY
S. gigantea: evergreen basal clumps of leaves, with oat-like flowers on long, arching stems.

STIPA TENUISSIMA
(syn. *Nassella tenuissima*)
♦ 0.6m (24in)
⊃ 0.45m (18in)
☼ ◑ ☐ ▢

Ponytail grass. Dense tussock-forming evergreen grass composed of thin stems and long filamentous flowers and seed heads. Indispensable for prairie-style plantings, especially in small spaces or border edges, it is attractive at all times of year. Comb out old growth in spring. Will self-seed.

bulbs

Whether naturalised in bold drifts or used as the ultimate seasonal companion plants, bulbs rarely disappoint. They provide cheery floral highlights, require little or no care and, when happy, will also spread to intensify the display.

ALLIUM
⋔ 0.15–1.2m (6in–4ft)
⬐ 0.15–0.5m (6–20in)
☼ ◑ ☐ ▣

Small to tall, spring to late summer-flowering bulbs. The spherical or pendant flower heads in purple, blue, pink, yellow or white, are valuable for pollinators. Many have attractive seed heads. Use in borders, gravel and pots.
RECOMMENDED VARIETY
A. hollandicum 'Purple Sensation': tall form, purple globes and good seed heads.

ANEMONE BLANDA
⋔ 0.05–0.1m (2–4in)
⬐ 0.05–0.1m (2–4in)
☼ ◑ ☐ ▣

Winter windflower. Gently spreading, mat-forming, semi-evergreen perennial for sunny or shady areas. Small daisy-like flowers in shades of blue, pink or white appear from early spring above dissected foliage. Ideal for naturalising around trees and shrubs.
RECOMMENDED VARIETY
A. b. 'Radar': bold, purple-pink flowers.

CAMASSIA
⋔ 0.3–1.5m (1–5ft)
⬐ 0.1–0.5m (4–20in)
☼ ◑ ☐ ▣ ■

Quamash. Bulbs with strap-shaped leaves and spires studded with star-shaped flowers from mid-spring. Displays of the blue, lilac, cream or white flowers are spectacular, but fleeting. Foliage dies away by summer. Will naturalise and is useful for short and rough grassland.
RECOMMENDED VARIETY
C. quamash: shortest species with rich purple-blue flowers.

⋔ HEIGHT   **⬐** SPREAD
☼ FULL SUN   ☐ DRY
◑ PART SUN   ▣ NORMAL
✸ SHADE   ■ DAMP

COLCHICUM
⋔ 0.1–0.2m (4–8in)
⬐ 0.1–0.2m (4–8in)
☼ ☐ ▣

Meadow saffron. Late summer and autumn-flowering bulbs with long-tubed chalices in lilac, pink and white. The broad leaves appear after flowering, and the whole plant dies down by midsummer. Good for naturalising in short, open grassland. Bulbs are toxic.
RECOMMENDED VARIETY
C. speciosum: rosy-pink flowers on strong stems. Will naturalise.

CROCUS
⋔ 0.1m (4in)
⬐ 0.1m (4in)
☼ ◑ ☐ ▣

Dwarf bulbs that produce goblet-shaped flowers in all colours from mid-winter to spring, although some flower in autumn. Good for pollinators. Stronger species and hybrids are ideal for naturalising in short grass; otherwise plant at border edges and around shrubs.
RECOMMENDED VARIETY
C. chrysanthus: fragrant flowers come in a wide range of colours. Will naturalise.

ERANTHIS HYEMALIS
⋔ 0.05–0.1m (2–4in)
⬐ 0.1m (4in)
☼ ◑ ☐ ▣

Winter aconite. Low ruffs of dissected foliage, each holding a yellow goblet-shaped flower in spring. The blooms are good for early pollinators. Use aconites to naturalise in moist soil – they tolerate drier conditions when dormant in summer. Ideal for areas beneath deciduous trees and shrubs. Plants die down by summer. Will self-seed when happy.

ERYTHRONIUM
⋔ 0.2–0.4m (8–16in)
⬐ 0.2–0.5m (8–20in)
◑ ☐ ▣

Dog's tooth violet. Bulbs with pairs of oval leaves, often mottled with maroon spots. Single-stalked or spires of pendant pink, lilac, yellow or white flowers with upswept petals appear in spring. Ideal for planting in drifts in semi-shade in moist, but not wet, soil. Some will naturalise.
RECOMMENDED VARIETY
E. dens-canis: a short species with single pink flowers and mottled leaves.

FRITILLARIA MELEAGRIS
♠ 0.1–0.5m (4–20in)
⬯ 0.1m (4in)
☼ ◐ ☐ ▪

Snake's-head fritillary. This British native bulb has narrow, upright foliage and pendant purple-pink or white bell-shaped spring flowers with a chequered pattern. Use it to decorate borders and pots or for naturalising in short mown grassland.

RECOMMENDED VARIETY
F. m. var *unicolor* sub var *alba*: white-flowered species.

GALANTHUS NIVALIS
♠ 0.1–0.15m (4–6in)
⬯ 0.1–0.15m (4–6in)
◐ ▪

Snowdrop. A British native bulb with strap-shaped leaves and pendant white late-winter flowers with green markings. Useful for early pollinators, it is easy to grow in moist, well-drained soil in semi-shade under deciduous trees or shrubs. Naturalises quickly.

RECOMMENDED VARIETY
G. nivalis f *pleniflorus* 'Flore Pleno': double–flowered form.

GLADIOLUS COMMUNIS SUBSP BYZANTINUS
♠ 0.4–0.6m (16–24in)
⬯ 0.15–0.3m (6–12in)
☼ ☐ ▪

Tall perennial corm with broad lance-shaped leaves. Spikes of funnel-shaped purple-red flowers appear from late spring. The hardiest gladiolus species for general garden use and for naturalising, even in open grassland. Best in a sheltered position in any moist, well-drained soil, it may not be fully hardy in cold climates.

HYACINTHOIDES NON–SCRIPTA
♠ 0.15–0.5m (6–20in)
⬯ 0.1–0.15m (4–6in)
◐ ☐ ▪

Bluebell. Clump-forming British native bulb with linear green leaves. Arching spikes of pendant blue scented flowers appear in spring. Grow it in moist, well-drained soil in semi-shade beneath deciduous trees and shrubs, or naturalise in short grassland. When happy, bluebells will colonise and spread quickly.

LEUCOJUM AESTIVUM
♠ 0.4–0.6m (16–24in)
⬯ 0.4–0.6m (16–24in)
◐ ☐ ▪ ■

Summer snowdrop. Tall bulbous clump-forming perennial with linear leaves. Arching stems of pendant bell-like white flowers, tipped with green, appear in late spring. Best in moist but well-drained soil, even periodically wet. Will naturalise in open ground or grassland.

RECOMMENDED VARIETY
L. a. 'Gravetye Giant': large variant of the species, good for naturalising.

NARCISSUS
♠ 0.15–0.45m (6–18in)
⬯ 0.15–0.3m (6–12in)
☼ ◐ ▪ ■

Daffodil. Clump-forming bulbs with long strap-shaped leaves. Yellow cup-and-saucer-shaped flowers in shades of yellow, orange and white appear over a long period in spring. Ideal for borders, naturalising in grassland, or planting around deciduous trees.

RECOMMENDED VARIETY
N. 'Mount Hood': pure white daffodil, becoming creamy yellow in the throat.

NECTAROSCORDUM SICULUM
♠ 1.2m (4ft)
⬯ 0.3m (12in)
☼ ◐ ☐ ▪

Honey garlic. This stout-stemmed, onion-relative produces heads of dangling olive, cream and red-banded flowers in late spring. Sweetly scented and a magnet for bees, its exotic-looking, erect seed pods last until late summer. Useful for threading through emerging grasses and herbaceous perennials. Will naturalise in open ground.

SCILLA SIBERICA
♠ 0.2m (8in)
⬯ 0.05m (2in)
☼ ◐ ☐ ▪

Siberian squill. Upright tufts of linear leaves form sheathes around short spikes of blue and white bell-shaped flowers in early spring. Good for planting around shrubs or along border edges, or use it for naturalising in semi-shade or full sun. This bulb prefers moist but well-drained soil, and, when happy, it will quickly colonise areas.

climbers

Whether clothing unsightly walls or cloaking narrow spaces where shrubs may not fit, climbers are essential garden plants. Their flowers are valuable for pollinators, while the tangled stems and leaves provide nesting sites for many garden birds.

○ HEIGHT   ⤺ SPREAD
☼ FULL SUN   ☐ DRY
☽ PART SUN   ▨ NORMAL
✺ SHADE   ■ DAMP

CAMPSIS
○ 2–8m (6ft 6in–26ft)
⤺ 2.5–4m (8–13ft)
☼ ☽ ▨
Deciduous climber with divided foliage and clusters of tubular flowers in shades of orange, yellow and red from midsummer onwards. Tie in stems to a wall or fence to establish the tiny clinging roots. Needs a warm spot; not fully hardy in cold climates.
RECOMMENDED VARIETY
C. x *tagliabuana* 'Madame Galen': orangey-red flowers.

CLEMATIS (SMALL-FLOWERED)
○ 1.2–6m (4–20ft)
⤺ 1–6m (39in–20ft)
☼ ☽ ✺ ▨
Deciduous, occasionally evergreen climbers, with some in flower almost all year. They cling via twining leaf-stalks, so need supporting trellis, wires or plants. Their nodding bells or star-shaped flowers come in many colours.
RECOMMENDED VARIETY
C. tangutica: nodding yellow flowers from late summer, and decorative fluffy seed heads.

HEDERA HELIX
○ 0.9–8m (36in–26ft)
⤺ 0.3–10m+ (12in–33ft)
☼ ☽ ✺ ☐ ▨
Ivy. Evergreen self-clinging climber with vast range of foliage shapes, and variegated and golden-leaved forms. Flowers produced on mature shoots provide a valuable late food source for pollinators, while the seeds are good for birds. Grow in any soil and aspect but use coloured leaf forms in shade to avoid scorch.

HYDRANGEA ANOMALA SUBSP PETIOLARIS
○ 4–12m (13–39ft)
⤺ 4–8m (13–26ft)
☽ ✺ ▨
Climbing hydrangea. Self-clinging deciduous climber with green simple leaves. Cinnamon shoots and white lace-cap flowers appear from late spring, followed by attractive seed heads. The plant has good autumn foliage colour. Thriving in dense shade and any soil, as long as it's not too dry, it may be slow to start until fully attached to a wall or fence.

JASMINUM OFFICINALE
○ 2.5–8m (8–26ft)
⤺ 0.5–2.5m (20in–8ft)
☼ ☽ ☐ ▨
Jasmine. Fast-growing evergreen climber with dissected leaves. Sweetly scented tubular white flowers appear in clusters over a long period in summer. Although generally hardy, provide a warm, sheltered position and grow in moist, free-draining soil. Tie the stems into a framework and remove unwanted growth annually in spring.

LONICERA
○ 3–10m (10–33ft)
⤺ 1.5–4m (5–13ft)
☼ ☽ ✺ ☐ ▨
Honeysuckle. Twining deciduous or evergreen climbers. Clusters of tubular flowers, often sweetly scented, in yellow, orange, red and pink appear from late spring, followed by red berries. Attractive to pollinators. Grow in sun or shade, and any soil as long as it's not too dry.
RECOMMENDED VARIETY
L. periclymenum 'Graham Thomas': white and cream highly fragrant flowers.

CLIMBING AND RAMBLING ROSES (SINGLE-FLOWERED)
○ 3–10m (10–33ft)
⤺ 3m+ (10ft+)
☼ ☽ ▨
Scrambling, thorny deciduous lax-stemmed climbing shrubs. Open disc-shaped flowers in many colours, often sweetly scented, appear from late spring onwards and offer a valuable food source for pollinators. Train and tie in stems to supports.
RECOMMENDED VARIETY
R. 'Francis E. Lester': pink-edged white fragrant flowers, and orange hips in autumn.

ACER
🎧 1.2–10m+ (4–33ft+)
🔄 1.2–10m+ (4–33ft+)
☼ ❂ ☐ ▬

Maple. Highly decorative and shapely, these predominantly deciduous trees look good at all times of year. Many have ornamental bark and most offer autumn colour. Many cast light shade and can be underplanted. Japanese maples, A. *palmatum* require moisture.

RECOMMENDED VARIETY

A. *campestre*: a versatile British native, good for wildlife.

trees & shrubs

All gardens, whatever their size, will benefit from the many virtues of trees and shrubs. They provide structure and shelter which, combined with their decorative leaves, flowers and fruit, are also of huge benefit to many forms of wildlife.

🛈 HEIGHT   ⮂ SPREAD

☼ FULL SUN   ▢ DRY

◑ PART SUN   ▬ NORMAL

✹ SHADE   ■ DAMP

ALNUS
🛈 10–20m+ (33–66ft+)
⮂ 4–8m (13–26ft)
☼ ◑ ▢ ▬ ■

Alder. Durable and versatile deciduous trees, tolerant of exposure and wet soils. Alders generate nitrogen in their roots, so are good for poor soil. Male and female catkins appear from late winter. Slow-growing cut-leaved forms are ideal for small plots.
RECOMMENDED VARIETY
A. glutinosa 'Laciniata': cut leaves and conical habit.

BERBERIS
🛈 0.5–4m (20in–13ft)
⮂ 0.5–4m (20in–13ft)
☼ ◑ ▢ ▬

Deciduous to evergreen shrubs with thorny stems and small leaves. Small flowers in yellow, cream or orange appear in spring and are good for pollinators. Attractive autumn fruit follows. Ideal for hedges and clipped forms, they will grow in most soils.
RECOMMENDED VARIETY
B. x stenophylla: evergreen form with yellow flowers.

BUDDLEJA
🛈 1.2–8m (4–26ft)
⮂ 1.5–8m (5–26ft)
☼ ◑ ▢ ▬

Buddleia. Fast growing deciduous to evergreen shrubs with sweetly–scented flower spikes in many shades. Very attractive to pollinators, especially butterflies, they grow in any soil, apart from wet. B. davidii is invasive.
RECOMMENDED VARIETY
B. 'Blue Chip': compact variety with blue flowers, ideal for pots. Not invasive.

CORNUS ALBA
🛈 2m (6ft 6in)
⮂ 2m (6ft 6in)
☼ ◑ ▬ ■

Dogwood. Deciduous suckering shrub with upright colourful stems in yellow, red and orange. Clusters of white flowers appear in late spring, followed by white berries. It offers autumn colour and winter effects in borders, naturalistic plantings and pond margins. Prune to generate new colourful stems.
RECOMMENDED VARIETY
C. a. 'Baton Rouge': striking pink-red winter stems.

COTONEASTER
🛈 1–8m (39in–26ft)
⮂ 0.5–8m (20in–26ft)
☼ ◑ ▢ ▬

Deciduous to evergreen shrubs with a diverse range of growth habits. The white spring flowers are attractive to pollinators and followed in autumn by red, orange or yellow berries. Deciduous species often have autumn tints. Some taller species can be trained into tree forms or clipped to make hedges.
RECOMMENDED VARIETY
C. 'Exburiensis': arching, tree-like hybrid with yellow berries.

CYTISUS
🛈 0.1–1.5m (4in–5ft)
⮂ 0.5–1.5m (20in–5ft)
☼ ▢

Broom. Small shrubs that bear evergreen stems with tiny, deciduous leaves. Masses of small pea-like flowers bloom in spring and are loved by pollinators. Able to generate nitrogen via bacteria in the root nodules, plants are good for poor, dry soil. Ideal for rock and Mediterranean-style gardens and sloping sites.
RECOMMENDED VARIETY
C. x praecox: rounded habit, with pale yellow blooms.

ELAEAGNUS
🛈 2.5m (8ft)
⮂ 2.5–4m (8–13ft)
☼ ◑ ▢ ▬

Oleaster. Vigorous, twiggy evergreen or deciduous shrubs, with many different habits. Tolerant of exposure and poor soil, they make good shelter belts and hedging. Tiny white, sweetly scented flowers appear from late summer, followed by edible berries. Silver-leaved types are drought tolerant.
RECOMMENDED VARIETY
E. x ebbingei: rounded habit, and grey leaves.

HEBE
🡙 0.1–2.5m (4in–8ft)
🡘 0.1–2.5m (4in–8ft)
☼ ◐ ☐ ▣
Mat or mound-forming evergreen shrubs with small, thick leaves, often coloured, especially in winter. Spikes of flowers in blue, mauve, pink or white appear in summer and are attractive to pollinators. Use in beds or gravel gardens. Not all are fully hardy.
RECOMMENDED VARIETY
H. subalpina: compact form with white flowers in summer.

HYSSOPUS OFFICINALIS
🡙 0.2–0.5m (8–20in)
🡘 0.5–1m (20–39in)
☼ ◐ ☐ ▣
Hyssop. Small, spreading semi-evergreen shrub with aromatic, linear leaves. Its spikes of blue two-lipped summer flowers are attractive to bees and other pollinators. Plants prefer well-drained, chalky soil; use them in gravel gardens or pots. Cut out old growth in spring.
RECOMMENDED VARIETIES
H. officinalis f *albus*: white form.

ILEX AQUIFOLIUM
🡙 10m+ (33ft+)
🡘 4–8m (13–26ft)
☼ ◐ ● ☐
English holly. Large evergreen shrub or medium-sized tree, with spiny, glossy leaves, some variegated. Flowers and berries are valuable for wildlife but berries are only produced on female or self-fertile varieties. Tolerant of exposure and most soils, and full sun to deep shade.
RECOMMENDED VARIETIES
I. a. 'Alaska': red berries.

LAVANDULA
🡙 0.3–1.4m (12in–4ft 5in)
🡘 0.2–0.9m (8–36in)
☼ ☐ ▣
Lavender. Tufted or mound-forming shrubs with aromatic grey leaves. The scented summer flower spikes in blue, purple, pink or white attract pollinators, especially bees. Grow in well-drained soil, in borders, gravel or large pots.
RECOMMENDED VARIETY
L. angustifolia 'Hidcote': compact variety with grey leaves and violet-blue flowers.

MAHONIA
🡙 0.5–4m (20in–13ft)
🡘 1.5–4m (5–13ft)
☼ ◐ ● ☐ ▣ ■
Mound-forming or tall upright evergreen shrubs with ruffs of spiny green foliage. Spires of yellow scented flowers appear in winter and spring, and are a useful food source for early pollinators. They provide striking architectural forms, especially in winter. Easy to grow in many conditions.
RECOMMENDED VARIETY
M. x media 'Charity': yellow, scented flowers and spiny foliage on upright stems.

MALUS
🡙 4–8m (13–26ft)
🡘 4–6m (13–20ft)
☼ ☐
Crab apple. Small, deciduous trees with variable habits. Spring displays of apple blossom and colourful fruit in autumn make it a good wildlife species. The flowers will often help pollinate varieties of eating apple too, and some have edible fruit, ideal for jams.
RECOMMENDED VARIETIES
M. 'Golden Hornet': white flowers followed by yellow fruit; 'John Downie': pink blooms, orange-red edible fruit.

PEROVSKIA ATRIPLICIFOLIA
🡙 1–1.5m (39in–5ft)
🡘 0.5–1m (20–39in)
☼ ◐ ☐ ▣
Russian sage. Bushy semi-woody shrub with narrow, toothed, grey aromatic leaves. Upright spires of violet-blue flowers appear from late summer offering a good food source for pollinators. Tolerant of semi-shade, grow it in well-drained soil in borders, naturalistic plantings, gravel and coastal gardens.
RECOMMENDED VARIETY
P. a. 'Blue Spire': striking branched flower stems.

PRUNUS
🡙 4–10m (13–33ft)
🡘 4–10m (13–33ft)
☼ ◐ ☐
Cherry. Deciduous trees with decorative spring blossom. Sizes and habits vary from large shrubs to medium-sized spreading trees. The flowers range from white to deep pink. Some also have vibrant autumn colour. The large wild cherry *P. avium*, medium-sized bird cherry *P. padus*, and shrubby sloe *P. spinosa* are all good for pollinators, birds and other wildlife. Grow in well-drained soil.

PYRACANTHA
🛈 1.5–4m (5–13ft)
➲ 1.5–4m (5–13ft)
☼ ◑ ☐ ◼

Firethorn. Large, densely-branched, spiny, evergreen shrubs. Robust and tolerant of most soils and exposure, use them as shelter belts, hedges, and wall shrubs. Their small white spring flowers, colourful berries in autumn and thorny stems are valuable for wildlife.

RECOMMENDED VARIETIES
P. 'Mohave': orange-red berries; 'Soleil d'Or': yellow berries.

ROSE (SINGLE FLOWERED)
🛈 1.5–4m (5–13ft)
➲ 1.5–2.5m (5–8ft)
☼ ◑ ◼

Mounding or upright spiny stemmed deciduous shrubs. Disc- or cup-shaped blooms in many colours, often scented, appear from late spring. Red or yellow hips follow in autumn. Attractive to pollinators, roses are ideal for borders and naturalistic plantings.

RECOMMENDED VARIETY
R. moyesii 'Geranium': red flowers and orange-red hips.

ROSMARINUS
🛈 0.1–2.5m (4in–8ft)
➲ 0.5–2.5m (20in–8ft)
☼ ☐ ◼

Rosemary. Prostrate to upright evergreen shrubs with narrow, highly aromatic leaves. A valuable early food source for pollinators, blue, pink or white hooded flowers form in mid-spring. Use them for borders, in gravel or pots, or as hedging.

RECOMMENDED VARIETY
R. officinalis 'Severn Sea': spreading habit with bright blue spring flowers.

SORBUS
🛈 8–15m (26–50ft)
➲ 4–10m (13–33ft)
☼ ◑ ☐ ◻ ◼

Whitebeam/rowan. Able to withstand exposure and grow in any soil, even wet, the British native whitebeam, S. aria, has oval foliage, while the rowan, S. aucuparia has finely divided leaves. Both produce red autumn berries and leaf colour. Other species have different coloured berries.

RECOMMENDED VARIETY
S. a. var edulis: edible red fruit.

SPIRAEA
🛈 0.6–2.5m (2–8ft)
➲ 0.6–2.5m (2–8ft)
☼ ◑ ☐ ◼

Bridal wreath. Twiggy, deciduous shrubs with clusters of white or pink flowers from late spring into summer, depending on species and variety. Easy to grow in most well-drained soils, and a useful filler among other shrubs. Lightly trim back after the flowers have finished.

RECOMMENDED VARIETIES
S. japonica 'Goldflame': yellow foliage, pink flowers; S. x vanhouttei: white blooms.

THYMUS
🛈 0.1–0.5m (4–20in)
➲ 0.1–0.5m (4–20in)
☼ ☐

Thyme. Carpeting to small, upright subshrubs, with highly aromatic, often colourful or grey foliage. Small blue, pink or white flowers appear from early summer and are attractive to pollinators. Grow in well-drained soil and sun on path or border edges, or in gravel gardens or pots.

RECOMMENDED VARIETY
T. pseudolanuginosus: forms mats of grey, woolly foliage with pink flowers in summer.

VIBURNUM
🛈 1–8m (39in–26ft)
➲ 1–4m (39in–13ft)
☼ ◑ ✷ ☐ ◻ ◼

Versatile deciduous or evergreen shrubs, with a wide range of foliage forms and growth habits. White or pink flowers, often scented and loved by pollinators, form in clusters from winter to midsummer. Leaves offer autumn colour and red berries provide food for birds.

RECOMMENDED VARIETY
V. sargentii 'Onondaga': deciduous, with white flowers, red berries and autumn tints.

WEIGELA
🛈 1.2–2.5m (4–8ft)
➲ 1.2–2.5m (4–8ft)
☼ ◑ ✷ ☐ ◼

Vigorous, fast-growing, deciduous shrubs, producing clusters of tubular flowers in shades of red, pink, yellow or white from early summer. The blooms attract many pollinators. Coloured and variegated leaved forms are more compact and slower-growing. Grow on well-drained soil, and prune after flowering.

RECOMMENDED VARIETY
W. middendorffiana: compact form with yellow flowers.

water & bog plants

The transition from water to land encompasses many exciting plant species. With such a wide range on offer for water and damp soils, take the opportunity to create something really special. The planting depths given here are measured from the water surface to the top of the root ball.

⋂ HEIGHT   ⮂ SPREAD
☼ FULL SUN   ☐ DRY
� PART SUN   ▣ NORMAL
✹ SHADE   ■ DAMP

Deep water

APONOGETON DISTACHYOS
⋂ 0.1m (4in)
⮂ 0.5–1m (20–39in)
☼ � ■

Water hawthorn. Submerged deciduous or semi-evergreen aquatic plant with a rhizomatous rootstock and floating elliptical leaves. Heads of small white flowers appear in spring and late summer just above the water surface. The flowers are edible. Plant 0.3–0.9m (12-36in) below the water surface.

NYMPHAEA
⋂ 0.1m (4in)
⮂ 0.3–1.8m+ (12in–6ft)
☼ � ■

Water lily. Rhizomatous deciduous aquatics with floating heart-shaped leaves and bowl-shaped flowers in red, yellow, and pink in summer. Varieties of different sizes and vigour are available.

RECOMMENDED VARIETY
N. 'Pygmaea Helvola': dwarf form; yellow fragrant flowers. Plant 10cm (4in) below surface.

NYMPHOIDES PELTATA
⋂ 0.1m (4in)
⮂ 1.2–1.8m (4–6ft)
☼ ■

Yellow floating heart. Floating deciduous aquatic with heart-shaped, mottled leaves. Yellow fringed flowers appear just above the water in summer. Tolerant of water depths from just submerged to 80cm (30in) deep, it will soon cover small ponds, so constrain in pots. Helps keep water clean and algae free.

Marginal/bog plants

ALISMA PLANTAGO-AQUATICA
⋂ 0.5–1m (20–39in)
⮂ 0.1–0.5m (4–20in)
☼ ■

Water plantain. Vigorous perennial with rosettes of large, spear-shaped, blue-green leaves. Large airy white or pink flower heads appear in summer; deadhead to prevent self-seeding. Plants spread by creeping rhizomes and will take over small ponds unless grown in a pot. Set in water up to 30cm (12in) deep.

ASTILBE
⋂ 0.3–2.5m (12in–8ft)
⮂ 0.3–1m (12–39in)
☼ � ▣ ■

Clump-forming upright deciduous or semi-evergreen perennials with filigree foliage. Frothy plumes of flowers in red, mauve, pink and white form in summer. Plant in moist soil in bog gardens, pond margins and damp borders.

RECOMMENDED VARIETY
A. 'Fanal': red plumes over dark green leaves.

BUTOMUS UMBELLATUS
⋂ 1–1.5m (39in–5ft)
⮂ 0.15–0.5m (6–20in)
☼ � ■

Flowering rush. Herbaceous aquatic perennial with slender, triangular leaves. Sprays of pink flowers on long stems appear in summer and are attractive to many pollinators, including butterflies. Submerge at a depth of 5–30cm (2–12in).

RECOMMENDED VARIETY
B. u. 'Schneeweisschen': blush pink flowers with red eyes.

CALTHA PALUSTRIS
⋂ 0.1–0.5m (4–20in)
⮂ 0.1–0.5m (4–20in)
☼ ☽ ■

Marsh marigold. Herbaceous clump-forming perennials with heart-shaped leaves. The cup-shaped yellow or white spring flowers are valuable for early pollinators. Will grow in wet soil or submerged in water up to 20cm (8ins) deep.

RECOMMENDED VARIETY
C. palustris var alba: white-flowered variant of species.

DARMERA PELTATA
◐ 0.6–1.5m (2–5ft)
➲ 0.6–1.2m (2–4ft)
☼ ◐ ■

Umbrella plant. Creeping herbaceous perennial with huge parasol-shaped leaves on long stems. Clusters of pink flowers appear before the leaves in late spring. Plant with rhizomes exposed in wet soil in a bog garden or pond side.

RECOMMENDED VARIETY
D. p. 'Nana': miniature form for smaller ponds.

FILIPENDULA
◐ 0.5–2.5m (20in–8ft)
➲ 0.3–1m (12–39in)
☼ ◐ ▭ ■

Meadowsweet. Deciduous perennials, including short to tall varieties, with ferny foliage below frothy summer flowers in cream or pink. Good for pollinators. Adaptable, but best in sun and moist soils in bog gardens or pond sides.

RECOMMENDED VARIETY
F. ulmaria : hip-height, with frothy cream summer flowers.

IRIS (AQUATIC FORMS)
◐ 0.4–1.5m (16in–5ft)
➲ 0.4–1.5m+ (16in–5ft+)
☼ ◐ ■

Rhizomatous perennials with 'fleur de lys' blooms in many shades from late spring. Bog and aquatic species include: vigorous native I. pseudacorus (plant 20cm (8in) below water); I. ensata (plant in wet soil in a bog or pond edge); I. laevigata (plant in wet soil or submerged to 15cm (6in)); I. sibirica (plant in damp or wet soil).

LIGULARIA
◐ 0.5–1.8m (20in–6ft)
➲ 0.3-1m (12–39in)
☼ ◐ ▭ ■

Clump-forming perennials with bold, architectural, sometimes dark foliage. Spires or open heads of long-lasting yellow daisies appear in summer. They like damp soils, but are also good for borders or pots. Protect from slugs and snails.

RECOMMENDED VARIETY
L. przewalskii: jagged foliage, tall yellow spires.

LYSIMACHIA
◐ 0.1–1m (4–39in)
➲ 0.15–1m (6–39in)
☼ ◐ ▭ ■

Loosestrife. Perennials with creeping to upright stems and green or coloured leaves. Spikes of yellow or white flowers appear in summer, and are useful for pollinators. Vigorous species, such as L. punctata, can be invasive.

RECOMMENDED VARIETY
L. ephemerum: grey-green leaves with white flowers.

RHEUM
◐ 1–2.5m (39in–8ft)
➲ 0.5–2.5m (20in–8ft)
☼ ◐ ● ▭

Ornamental rhubarb. Clump-forming perennials with huge leaves and large heads of small summer flowers on stout stems. Imposing, architectural plants for moist soils in pool-side settings or bog gardens.

RECOMMENDED VARIETY
R. palmatum 'Atrosanguineum': red-tinged leaves and red flowers in summer.

RODGERSIA
◐ 1–1.8m (39in–6ft)
➲ 0.5–1.8m (20in–6ft)
☼ ◐ ▭ ■

Large perennials with bold lobed or toothed leaves, often veined, that lend a subtropical look. Young foliage is often tinted. Sprays of frothy white or pink flowers on long stalks appear in summer. They may be slow to establish.

RECOMMENDED VARIETY
R. pinnata: bold foliage, white/pink flowering spires.

TYPHA MINIMA
◐ 0.6m (24in)
➲ 0.6m (24in)
☼ ■

Dwarf reedmace. Evergreen creeping perennial species with upright stems topped by small, velvety-brown bobbled seed heads in summer. Ideal for small ponds and water gardens in containers. Submerge plants in pots or baskets 2.5cm (1in) below the water surface.

sourcebook

8

directory of useful contacts & suppliers

SEED MIXTURES & PLANT RETAILERS

BOSTON SEEDS
Wide range of seeds of many British native wildflowers and mixtures; seeds in commercial quantities; bulbs for naturalising; plugs and larger pots of native plant species also available.
www.bostonseeds.com

EMORSGATE SEEDS
Specialists in British native wildflowers, grass species and mixtures for domestic settings and conservation and general landscape use; consultancy also offered.
www.wildseed.co.uk

FLOWERSCAPES
Native and exotic seed mixtures for various sites and situations; mixtures for pollinators; seed quantites for medium to large scale gardens; plug plant mixtures; consultancy offered.
www.flowerscapes.org.uk

LEFT Meadow planting in a wild garden by Catherine Thomas (see p.170).

JOHN CHAMBERS WILDFLOWERS
Wide selection of British native wildflower species and wildflower mixtures for different habitats and purposes; quantities for domestic and commercial users.
www.johnchamberswildflowers.co.uk

MR FOTHERGILL'S SEEDS
Seed mixtures in small amounts for various situations; seed mixtures for pollinators; seed impregnated papers.
www.mr-fothergills.co.uk

NATIONAL WILDFLOWER CENTRE
Visitor centre and display gardens for the wildflower conservation charity Landlife (www.wildflower.co.uk). Seed mixes available for various uses and situations; publications on wildflower topics; events; consultancy on wildflower plantings available.
www.nwc.org.uk

PICTORIAL MEADOWS
Wide range of ornamental and native seed mixes for different effects and site conditions; quantities for both domestic and commercial users; events and demonstrations.
www.pictorialmeadows.co.uk

SUTTONS SEEDS
Seed mixtures in small amounts for various situations; seed mixtures for pollinators.
www.suttons.co.uk

THOMPSON & MORGAN
Seed mixtures in small amounts for various situations; seed mixtures for pollinators.
www.thompson-morgan.com

TREE & SHRUB SUPPLIERS

AGROFORESTRY RESEARCH TRUST
Selection of unusual fruit and edible woodland plants; information on agroforestry topics; events.
www.agroforestry.co.uk

BLACKMOOR NURSERIES
Wide range of fruit and ornamental trees.
www.blackmoor.co.uk

CHEW VALLEY TREES
Native, fruit and ornamental trees, shrubs and hedging plants.
www.chewvalleytrees.co.uk

CHRIS BOWERS
A broad range of fruit trees and shrubs, as well as soft fruits.
www.chrisbowers.co.uk

FRANK P MATTHEWS
Wide range of woody ornamentals, especially trees and fruit, with a good range of apples and other top fruit.
www.frankpmatthews.com

KEEPERS NURSERY
Wide selection of fruit and nut trees of local/regional provenance; rare varieties grafted to order.
www.keepers-nursery.co.uk

KEN MUIR
Wide range of fruit crops, especially soft fruit.
www.kenmuir.co.uk

POMONA FRUITS
Wide range of fruit trees of all kinds, as well as hedging plants.
www.pomonafruits.co.uk

READS NURSERY
Wide range of fruit trees of all kinds, especially grapes and figs; ornamental trees and shrubs.
www.readsnursery.co.uk

THORNHAYES
Wide range of ornamental trees and shrubs. Fruit trees, including apples, pears and cherries; hedging also available.
www.thornhayes-nursery.co.uk

HERBACEOUS PLANT SUPPLIERS

THE CONSERVATION VOLUNTEERS
Seeds, bulbs, herbaceous plant plugs and bare-root trees and shrubs of British native species; books and information on planting and garden-feature construction techniques.
www.tcv.org.uk

COTSWOLD GARDEN FLOWERS
Very wide selection of herbaceous perennials, bulbs and small shrubs, many unusual and available nowhere else.
www.cgf.net

HARDY'S COTTAGE GARDEN PLANTS
Wide range of herbaceous perennials suitable for naturalistic schemes and cottage garden-style plantings.
www.hardys-plants.co.uk

KNOLL NURSERY
Specialists in ornamental grasses and herbaceous plants for naturalistic schemes; demonstration garden; consultancy offered.
www.knollgardens.co.uk

BULB SUPPLIERS

AVON BULBS
Wide range of spring, summer, autumn and winter-flowering bulbs.
www.avonbulbs.co.uk

BLOMS BULBS
Offering a broad range of spring, summer, autumn and winter-flowering bulbs.
www.blomsbulbs.com

PETER NYSSEN
A wide range of bulbs for all seasons in small and bulk quantities for gardens and larger landscapes.
www.peternyssen.com

R V ROGER
Unusual bulbs, plus shrubs, fruit and ornamental trees.
www.rvroger.co.uk

WILDFLOWER TURF SUPPLIERS

MEADOWMAT
Range of turf mats impregnated with wildflower seed. Bespoke mixtures offered.
www.meadowmat.com

ROOF GARDENS AND GREEN WALLS

ENVIROMAT
Pre-grown sedum matting for easy-to-install green roofs.
www.enviromat.co.uk

GREEN ROOF SHELTERS
Provides help and advice to homeowners and professionals wanting to construct green roofs in domestic locations. Range of green roof structures for sale, and bespoke designs.
www.greenroofshelters.co.uk

WATERMATIC
Innovative irrigation and water harvesting systems; green wall and roof installations.
www.watermaticltd.co.uk

WILDFLOWER & WILDLIFE CHARITIES
Important sources of information and advice

BRITISH TRUST FOR ORNITHOLOGY
Research charity investigating the population movements and ecology of wild birds in the UK. Results of the research are published on their website.
www.bto.org

BUGLIFE
Conservation charity providing support and information on invertebrates, such as insects, spiders and earthworms. Offers workshops and professional consultations.
www.buglife.org.uk

BUMBLEBEE CONSERVATION TRUST
Conservation charity promoting the interests of bumblebees and their conservation in the UK. Provides information to the public and consultation services to professional organisations and individuals.
www.bumblebeeconservation.org

BUTTERFLY CONSERVATION
Conservation charity devoted to conserving UK butterflies and moths and their habitats. Active conservation projects, with over 30 nature reserves across the UK. Provides information to the public and consultation services and advice to professional bodies and individuals.
www.butterfly-conservation.org

THE COTTAGE GARDEN SOCIETY
Membership society devoted to conserving and actively promoting cottage gardening and cottage garden planting style. It has more than 35 groups around the UK, that stage programmes of lectures, events, garden visits and plant and seed swaps.
thecottagegardensociety.org.uk

FROGLIFE
Conservation charity supporting the interests of amphibians and reptiles in Britain and Ireland. Provides information both to the general public and professional bodies.
www.froglife.org

PLANTLIFE
Conservation and campaigning organisation supporting and promoting interest in wildflowers, plants and fungi of the UK. Lobbyists of government to further the conservation and cause of native UK flora. Undertakes practical conservation projects in meadows, heathland, and coastal habitats.
www.plantlife.org.uk

RSPB
Conservation charity and membership organisation promoting interest in and helping conserve birds and other wildlife in the UK. One of the largest environmental charities in Britain. Runs over 200 nature reserves and has many active conservation projects. Provides vast amounts of information and publications to the public. Provides consultation services to government, professional bodies and individuals.
www.rspb.org.uk

THE WILDLIFE TRUSTS
Charity dedicated to inspiring the public about the value and importance of the natural world and its diverse range of habitats and environments. Active conservation projects throughout the UK. Wide range of books, publications and local events.
www.wildlifetrusts.org

WOODLAND TRUST
The UK's largest woodland conservation charity actively campaigning to protect all types of native woodland and the wildlife communities they support. Projects to create new native woodland with the help of communities, organisations and schools. Wide range of publications and local activity days.
www.woodlandtrust.org.uk

garden designers

The following garden designers and landscape architects specialise
in wildlife-friendly schemes and naturalistic planting schemes.

ACRES WILD
Specialises in large country
gardens in the UK and
worldwide.
www.acreswild.co.uk

BUCKLEY DESIGN ASSOCIATES
Large and small gardens
designed by Declan Buckley.
www.buckleydesignassociates.com

CHERYL CUMMINGS GARDEN DESIGN
Large and small gardens
designed in South Wales and
the West Country.
www.gardendesignerwales.co.uk

HELEN ELKS-SMITH LANDSCAPE AND GARDEN DESIGN
Garden and landscape design
in the South-East of England.
www.elks-smith.co.uk

FISHER TOMLIN & BOWYER
Large and small garden design,
and commercial projects,
throughout the UK
and worldwide.
www.andrewfishertomlin.com

THE GARDEN COMPANY
Large and small garden design
and construction, mainly in the
South-East of England.
www.thegardenco.co.uk

ANTHEA HARRISON GARDEN DESIGN
Gardens of all sizes and styles
designed in the South East
region of England.
www.antheaharrison.co.uk

LONDON GARDEN DESIGNER
Designs for large and small
gardens in London and South-East
of England by Sara Jane Rothwell.
www.londongardendesigner.com

MATT NICHOL GARDEN DESIGN
Gardens of all sizes designed
throughout the UK.
www.mngardendesign.co.uk

ULF NORDFJELL
Swedish designer of private
gardens and public spaces
througout Europe and worldwide.
www.nordfjellcollection.se

SARAH PRICE LANDSCAPES
Naturalistic planting and garden
designs throughout the UK.
www.sarahpricelandscapes.com

RICHARD ROMANG LANDSCAPE DESIGN
Garden design, and commercial
landscapes, throughout the UK.
www.richardromang.co.uk

SCAPE DESIGN
Large and small gardens designed
primarily in the South of France,
by James Basson.
www.scapedesign.com

FIONA STEPHENSON DESIGNS
Residential and commercial
projects throughout the UK
and worldwide.
www.fionastephensondesigns.com

TOM STUART-SMITH
Large private gardens and
public spaces throughout the UK
and worldwide.
www.tomstuartsmith.co.uk

CATHERINE THOMAS LANDSCAPE AND GARDEN DESIGN
Specialist in sustainable
landscapes and garden design
throughout the UK.
www.catherinethomas.co.uk

SUE TOWNSEND GARDEN DESIGN
Large and small gardens
designed in East Anglia and the
South-East of England.
suetownsendgardendesign.co.uk

SYLVAN STUDIO
Garden and landscape
design in South of England,
by Christine Whatley.
www.sylvanstudio.co.uk

CLEVE WEST LANDSCAPE DESIGN
Naturalistic planting and garden
design throughout the UK
and worldwide.
www.clevewest.com

RIGHT This beautiful naturalistic design
of grasses and late-flowering perennials,
including Japanese anemones, asters
and rudbeckias, is by James Scott of
The Garden Company.

index

Page numbers in *italics* indicate a caption for an illustration.
Page numbers in **bold** indicate a boxed entry, such as plant lists.
The Plant Gallery (pp.142–163) includes illustrations as
well as information

acknowledgements

I would like to thank Helen Griffin at Frances Lincoln for inviting me undertake the project and write the book. To Piet Oudolf, Professors James Hitchmough, Nigel Dunnett, the late Oliver Gilbert at Sheffield University, and Dr Wolfram Kirchner of Anhalt University, Germany. All provided inimitable creativity through their various inspired plantings and teachings over many years.

I would also like to thank photographer Neil Hepworth who diligently and faithfully recorded my forays into naturalistic gardening. Many thanks also to all those individuals who allowed us the use of images of their work, in particular Debbie Roberts and Ian Smith of Acres Wild; Andrew Fisher Tomlin of Fisher Tomlin & Bowyer; Cheryl Cummings; Matt Nichol; James Basson; Helen Elks-Smith; Anthea Harrison; James Scott of The Garden Company; Fiona Stephenson; Catherine Thomas; Christine Whatley of Sylvan Studio; Sue Townsend; and Dr Karin Alton of Flowerscapes. Thank you also to Karen Lynes of Peter Nyssen Limited for the supply of spring bulbs and images.

My gratitude also goes to Angela Lambert at Q Lawns (Meadowmat) and photographer David Wootton for assistance with the meadow turf project. My appreciation also to Zia Allaway, for editorial zeal and helping keep things on track, and to Becky Clarke for her inspired design. Finally, and by no-means least, to my wife, Judith, for unerring patience, support and encouragement throughout.

picture credits

t=top, b=bottom, m=middle, l=left, r=right, c=centre